# Xcode and SwiftUI Handbook

## A Complete guide to IOS App Development

## Benjamin E. Douglas

# TABLE OF CONTENTS

# Introduction

## The Evolution of iOS Development

The iOS development journey has undergone significant transformations since the launch of Apple's first iPhone in 2007. Initially, iOS apps were developed using Objective-C, a language steeped in tradition and commonly used for building software on Apple's platforms. However, over the years, the introduction of newer technologies and a shift in developer needs have prompted changes that have reshaped the iOS development ecosystem. Today, Swift, Apple's more modern and user-friendly programming language, alongside SwiftUI, has become the standard for building iOS apps. Understanding the evolution from Objective-C to Swift, and the adoption of SwiftUI, is crucial for developers aiming to stay ahead in this fast-evolving industry.

### From Objective-C to Swift

Objective-C was the primary programming language for iOS development for many years. It was powerful, but its syntax could be complex and unintuitive for beginners. Objective-C's reliance on pointers and manual memory management created a steep learning curve and was prone to errors. Despite these challenges, the language had its place in the iOS development ecosystem, providing flexibility and power, particularly for complex applications.

In 2014, Apple introduced **Swift** as a modern, safer, and more efficient alternative to Objective-C. Swift aimed to address the shortcomings of Objective-C by making the language easier to learn and more robust, particularly in terms of memory management. Swift incorporates many modern programming paradigms, such as optionals and closures, making it more concise and expressive. It also provides automatic memory management through **Automatic Reference Counting (ARC)**, eliminating the need for developers to manually manage memory, which can be error-prone and time-consuming.

Since its release, Swift has rapidly gained traction due to its simplicity, readability, and performance. Swift's features, such as type inference and error handling, help developers write cleaner and more maintainable code. Apple's strong commitment to Swift has made it a key language for iOS development, ensuring its place as the primary tool for modern app development on Apple platforms.

**Xcode: A Powerhouse for iOS Developers**

At the heart of iOS development is **Xcode**, Apple's integrated development environment (IDE). Xcode serves as the go-to tool for building, testing, and debugging iOS applications. Its rich set of features includes a code editor, graphical user interface (GUI) builder, simulator, and debugging tools, making it an all-in-one solution for developers.

Xcode provides a seamless environment for working with both Swift and Objective-C, but it truly shines when used with Swift. The editor in Xcode offers features such as auto-completion, real-time error checking, and suggestions for improving code, which enhance the coding experience and speed up development. The **Interface Builder** in Xcode allows developers to visually design user interfaces, making it easier to prototype apps without writing code for the UI from scratch.

Additionally, Xcode integrates tightly with the **Swift compiler**, allowing for fast and efficient building of Swift-based apps. The **Swift Package Manager** also simplifies dependency management, making it easier for developers to integrate third-party libraries into their projects.

Moreover, Xcode's powerful simulator provides a virtual environment where developers can test their apps on different iPhone and iPad models, ensuring compatibility across multiple devices without needing physical hardware. Xcode also offers **performance analysis tools**, which are essential for identifying performance bottlenecks and optimizing apps.

**Introduction to SwiftUI: The Future of Interface Design**

As iOS development progressed, Apple recognized the need for a more modern, efficient way to build user interfaces. This led to the development of **SwiftUI**, a framework introduced in 2019 that allows developers to create user interfaces using declarative syntax. Unlike UIKit, which requires developers to manipulate views and UI elements imperatively, SwiftUI makes it easier to design complex interfaces by describing what the UI should look like, rather than how it should be created.

With SwiftUI, developers can design user interfaces that automatically adapt to changes in device orientation, screen size, and platform. SwiftUI is also compatible across Apple's ecosystem, allowing apps to run seamlessly on iPhone, iPad, macOS, watchOS, and tvOS. This cross-platform functionality means that developers can write code once and run it across all devices, saving time and effort when creating apps for the Apple ecosystem.

SwiftUI's integration with **Combine**, Apple's reactive programming framework, further enhances its capabilities. With Combine, developers can easily bind data to UI components, enabling real-time updates when the data changes. This makes building dynamic, data-driven applications straightforward and efficient.

SwiftUI's emphasis on **reusable components** and **live previews** accelerates the development process by allowing developers to quickly see the effects of their changes. SwiftUI is designed to minimize the amount of code needed to create sophisticated user interfaces, making it a key tool for future iOS development.

**Why This Book is Different: An Advanced Approach to iOS Development**

There are many resources available for learning iOS development, but few provide the depth of knowledge required for professional developers seeking to master Swift, SwiftUI, and Xcode. This book stands out by offering an **advanced approach to iOS development**, focusing on the intricacies and best practices that make a developer truly proficient.

Unlike beginner-level books, which only scratch the surface of iOS development, this guide dives into the advanced aspects of **Swift**, **SwiftUI**, and **Xcode**, offering a comprehensive understanding of the tools and techniques necessary for building complex and scalable iOS applications. The book covers the full range of topics from **advanced Swift programming** concepts, such as protocols, closures, and error handling, to building high-performance, responsive UIs with SwiftUI.

Throughout this book, readers will learn not only how to use the tools, but also the **why** behind the design decisions that lead to high-quality apps. Each section includes practical examples, best practices, and strategies for overcoming common challenges, helping readers become more efficient and effective iOS developers.

One of the key differentiators of this book is its focus on **real-world applications**. The principles discussed are not just theoretical but are meant to be applied to actual development projects. Whether you're building an app for a startup or contributing to a large-scale enterprise solution, this book provides the skills and insights needed to develop polished, production-ready apps.

This book is not simply a guide to mastering the basics of iOS development; it's a roadmap for becoming an expert in the field, equipping developers with the knowledge and confidence to take on complex challenges in modern app development.

# Chapter 1

# Setting Up Your Development Environment

## Installing Xcode: Best Practices

Getting started with iOS development requires having the right tools in place, and **Xcode** is the cornerstone of this process. Xcode is Apple's official integrated development environment (IDE) for iOS and macOS application development, and it includes everything a developer needs to build, test, and deploy apps.

Before beginning the installation process, ensure that your Mac meets the minimum system requirements for the latest version of Xcode. Apple typically updates Xcode to correspond with the latest macOS version, so it's essential to check compatibility before downloading.

### Step-by-Step Installation Guide

1. **Download from the Mac App Store**
   The simplest way to install Xcode is through the Mac App Store. Open the **App Store** on your Mac, search for Xcode, and click the **Install** button. It may take some time, depending on your internet speed, as Xcode is a large file.

### Install Command Line Tools
During the installation process, you may also be prompted to install **Xcode Command Line Tools**. These tools are critical for performing certain tasks like

running scripts and managing development environments from the terminal. Install them by opening Terminal and running the following command:

xcode-select --install

2.

**Verify Installation**

After installation, open Xcode and ensure it runs properly. Check for any required updates and make sure everything is functioning as expected. You can verify the installation by running the following command in the terminal:

xcode-select -p

3. This command will display the location of the Xcode tools installed on your system.

**Best Practices for Maintaining Your Installation**

- **Regular Updates**: Xcode is frequently updated with new features, bug fixes, and performance improvements. Always keep your Xcode updated to take advantage of the latest enhancements. Updates can be managed directly through the Mac App Store.

- **Backup Projects**: Xcode occasionally undergoes significant updates, which may affect compatibility with older projects. Always back up your important codebases and projects before upgrading Xcode to ensure nothing is lost in the process.

- **Install Older Versions if Necessary**: In some cases, you may need an older version of Xcode to maintain compatibility with legacy projects. Apple provides the ability to download older versions of Xcode from the **Apple Developer** website.

# Xcode Versions and Compatibility

Each version of Xcode comes with its own set of features, improvements, and bug fixes, but also introduces compatibility considerations for both **macOS** and **iOS** projects. Understanding these compatibility aspects is crucial for smooth development across different versions.

### Current and Legacy Support

Xcode works in tandem with the iOS and macOS versions it supports. Every new version of Xcode is typically optimized to support the latest versions of iOS, macOS, and other Apple platforms. However, developers must be cautious when working with legacy systems or supporting older devices.

For instance, when working with **Xcode 12**, developers should be aware that **iOS 14** is the minimum supported operating system for building apps. If you're targeting older iOS versions like **iOS 13**, using Xcode 11 or earlier would be a better choice.

### Checking Compatibility Before Upgrading

It's important to check the compatibility of your current projects with the latest Xcode version. When upgrading Xcode, sometimes projects need to be recompiled or require changes to work with newer Swift versions or APIs. Always refer to the official Apple documentation and community forums to learn about any known issues with upgrading.

# Essential Tools for Efficient Development

While **Xcode** provides an array of built-in tools, there are several essential third-party tools and libraries that can significantly enhance the iOS development workflow. These tools help streamline various aspects of development, from writing code to debugging and testing.

### Git for Version Control

Version control is vital for any development project, and **Git** is the most widely used system for managing changes in codebases. Xcode has built-in support for Git, allowing developers to perform common version control tasks such as committing changes, branching, and merging, directly within the IDE. Setting up a repository for your projects is straightforward and can be done using the **Source Control** feature in Xcode.

### CocoaPods and Swift Package Manager

Managing external libraries is another essential aspect of iOS development. **CocoaPods** is a dependency manager for Swift and Objective-C Cocoa projects, while **Swift Package Manager (SPM)** is Apple's official solution for managing Swift libraries. These tools make it easy to integrate and manage third-party libraries in your project, saving time and reducing the complexity of manual integration.

### Fastlane for Automation

Automating tasks like code signing, building, testing, and releasing apps can save a significant amount of time, especially in larger projects. **Fastlane** is an open-source tool that automates these processes, allowing developers to streamline their CI/CD pipeline. Integrating Fastlane into your workflow can help you focus on writing code rather than repetitive tasks.

## Navigating Xcode's Interface

Once Xcode is installed and set up, it's time to get familiar with the IDE's user interface. Xcode's interface is designed to be highly intuitive, but it's packed with features that require understanding to navigate efficiently.

### The Main Window

The main window of Xcode consists of several key components:

- **Editor Area**: This is where you write your code. It supports multiple editors, so you can view files side by side.

- **Navigator Area**: Located on the left, this area contains various views such as the **Project Navigator**, **Symbol Navigator**, **Find Navigator**, and others. These views provide quick access to different parts of your project.

- **Utilities Area**: On the right side, this area displays properties, quick actions, and additional information based on the selected file or item.

- **Toolbar**: The toolbar at the top contains essential controls like the **Build** and **Run** buttons, which allow you to test your app on a simulator or connected device.

**Using Interface Builder**

**Interface Builder** is Xcode's visual tool for designing user interfaces. With it, you can drag and drop components like buttons, text fields, and labels onto your app's screens. Interface Builder also integrates tightly with SwiftUI, allowing you to create declarative UIs using Swift code, but still providing visual aids for layout and structure.

# Project Navigator, Interface Builder, and the Debugging Tools

In Xcode, the **Project Navigator** is an essential tool for organizing and managing your project files. It provides a tree-like structure for accessing all the resources and code within your project. Whether you are looking for Swift files, images, or XIB files, the Project Navigator allows you to locate them quickly and efficiently.

**Debugging Tools**

Xcode comes equipped with several powerful debugging tools:

- **LLDB Debugger**: The **LLDB** debugger provides developers with detailed insights into their app's execution. It supports breakpoints, watchpoints, and detailed inspection of variables and memory.

- **Console Output**: The console shows runtime logs and errors, which are crucial for identifying bugs and issues within the app.

- **View Debugger**: The View Debugger allows developers to visualize the structure of their app's UI at runtime. It displays a 3D representation of the app's views and allows you to inspect the properties of each component.

## Advanced Configuration and Workflow Customization

Xcode is highly customizable, and developers can optimize their workflows by configuring the IDE to fit their specific needs.

### Customizing the Layout

Xcode allows developers to adjust the workspace layout to suit their preferences. You can customize the size and position of various panels, such as the editor, navigator, and utilities area, to maximize productivity. You can also set up **multiple editors** to view different files simultaneously, which is helpful when working on large projects.

### Keyboard Shortcuts and Code Snippets

Using keyboard shortcuts can significantly speed up development. Xcode supports a wide array of shortcuts, and developers can customize them to improve workflow. Additionally, you can create and use **code snippets** to quickly insert commonly used blocks of code into your project.

## SwiftUI vs UIKit: Understanding the Core Difference

When developing iOS apps, developers must choose between **SwiftUI** and **UIKit**, two frameworks for building user interfaces. While both serve similar purposes, they differ significantly in how they approach UI design.

### UIKit

UIKit is the traditional framework for building iOS user interfaces, relying on an imperative approach. Developers must manually define the layout, position, and behavior of UI elements. While UIKit offers extensive control and customization, it can be time-consuming and error-prone, especially for complex UIs.

**SwiftUI**

SwiftUI, on the other hand, uses a declarative syntax, meaning developers describe the layout and behavior of the interface, and SwiftUI handles the details. SwiftUI enables rapid development and is ideal for creating modern, dynamic interfaces with less code. It also integrates seamlessly with Combine for reactive programming, allowing UI updates in response to data changes.

## Choosing the Right Framework for Your Project

The decision between SwiftUI and UIKit depends largely on the requirements of the project. SwiftUI is a powerful tool for building new, modern applications, especially for those targeting iOS 13 and later. It is ideal for applications that require a clean, dynamic user interface. UIKit, however, remains a robust choice for more complex and legacy applications, offering finer control over UI elements and better compatibility with older versions of iOS.

## Working with Mixed Projects (SwiftUI + UIKit)

It's not always necessary to choose between SwiftUI and UIKit, as both frameworks can coexist within the same project. In some cases, you may prefer to use SwiftUI for the main interface while retaining UIKit for complex legacy views or functionalities that haven't yet been ported to SwiftUI. Integrating SwiftUI views into a UIKit project is straightforward, and vice versa, thanks to Apple's interoperability features.

Using both frameworks in the same project allows you to leverage the strengths of each while maintaining compatibility with older iOS versions or complex components. However, it requires a careful approach to ensure that the interaction between the two frameworks remains seamless and doesn't introduce unexpected bugs.

# Chapter 2

# Fundamentals of Swift and SwiftUI

## Core Swift Concepts Every Developer Must Know

Swift, Apple's powerful and intuitive programming language, is the foundation of iOS and macOS development. Understanding the core concepts of Swift is essential for every developer, as it provides the building blocks for all iOS app development. In this section, we'll explore the fundamental concepts that every developer must be familiar with to become proficient in Swift.

### Variables, Constants, and Data Types

In Swift, managing data starts with understanding variables and constants. Variables are used to store values that may change over time, while constants are used for values that remain fixed. Both are declared with type annotations, though Swift's type inference often makes explicit type declarations unnecessary.

```
var age: Int = 25     // Variable
let pi: Double = 3.14159  // Constant
```

Swift supports various data types, including **Int**, **Double**, **String**, and **Bool**, and offers powerful type safety, ensuring that only the correct type of data can be assigned to a variable or constant.

### Control Flow: Conditionals and Loops

Control flow structures such as **if-else statements**, **switch cases**, and **for-in loops** are essential for directing the flow of an application. Swift's **switch** statement is especially powerful, supporting multiple conditions and complex patterns, making it more flexible than traditional if-else chains.

```
let number = 2
switch number {
case 1:
   print("One")
case 2:
   print("Two")
default:
   print("Other")
}
```

Loops are used to perform repetitive tasks, and Swift provides various loop structures, including the traditional **for-in**, **while**, and **repeat-while** loops.

**Optionals: Handling Missing Values**

In Swift, **optionals** are used to represent a variable that might not have a value. An optional either holds a value or is `nil`. Optionals are declared with a question mark (?), and their values are safely unwrapped using either optional binding or optional chaining.

```
var name: String? = "John"
if let unwrappedName = name {
   print("Hello, \(unwrappedName)!")
} else {
   print("Name is nil.")
}
```

Understanding optionals is critical for handling cases where data might be absent or unavailable, a common scenario in app development, particularly when interacting with APIs or databases.

## Functions, Closures, and Optionals in Depth

Swift provides robust support for **functions**, **closures**, and advanced handling of **optionals**, which allow developers to write clean, efficient, and safe code.

### Functions: Defining and Calling

A function is a self-contained block of code that performs a specific task. Functions can accept parameters and return values, making them extremely versatile in various programming tasks.

```swift
func greet(name: String) -> String {
    return "Hello, \(name)!"
}
print(greet(name: "Alice"))  // Output: Hello, Alice!
```

Swift also supports **multiple return values**, allowing functions to return tuples, making it easy to return multiple related values in a single call.

```swift
func getCoordinates() -> (x: Int, y: Int) {
    return (10, 20)
}
let coordinates = getCoordinates()
print("x: \(coordinates.x), y: \(coordinates.y)")
```

### Closures: Anonymous Functions

Closures are self-contained blocks of code that can be passed around and used in your code. They can capture and store references to variables and constants from the surrounding context, known as **capturing values**.

Closures are often used in places where you need a block of code that doesn't necessarily need to be named, such as in callbacks or asynchronous operations.

```swift
let addClosure = { (a: Int, b: Int) -> Int in
    return a + b
```

```
}
print(addClosure(3, 5))  // Output: 8
```

### Advanced Optional Handling

In addition to basic optional binding, Swift provides several ways to safely handle optionals. **Optional chaining** allows you to query and call properties, methods, and subscripts on optional values without explicitly unwrapping them, thus avoiding runtime errors.

```
let person: Person? = getPerson()
let name = person?.name  // Safely access name, if person is not nil
```

Swift also supports **nil-coalescing**, which provides a default value when an optional is `nil`.

```
let name = person?.name ?? "Unknown"
```

## Swift's Advanced Data Structures and Algorithms

To build more efficient and scalable iOS apps, it's essential to understand how to leverage **advanced data structures** and **algorithms** in Swift.

### Arrays and Dictionaries

Swift's **Array** and **Dictionary** are powerful, type-safe collections that allow you to store ordered and key-value data, respectively. Both collections support methods for adding, removing, and manipulating data.

```
var numbers: [Int] = [1, 2, 3]
numbers.append(4)
```

```
var capitals: [String: String] = ["USA": "Washington, D.C.", "Canada": "Ottawa"]
capitals["UK"] = "London"
```

### Sets and Tuples

A **Set** is an unordered collection of unique values, useful for eliminating duplicates from an array. Swift also supports **tuples**, which allow you to store multiple values of different types in a single compound value.

var uniqueNumbers: Set = [1, 2, 3, 3, 2]  // [1, 2, 3]

### Algorithms

Swift provides a rich set of algorithms through the **Swift Standard Library**. For example, you can sort an array using the `sorted()` method or search for elements with `contains()`.

let sortedNumbers = numbers.sorted()

You can also implement more advanced algorithms, such as sorting or searching algorithms, to optimize your application's performance when handling large datasets.

## Introduction to SwiftUI: The Power of Declarative Syntax

SwiftUI revolutionizes the way developers build user interfaces by providing a **declarative syntax** for UI creation. Unlike traditional imperative UI frameworks, SwiftUI allows developers to describe how the UI should look and behave in terms of state and data, and the framework takes care of updating the interface automatically when the data changes.

### What Makes SwiftUI Different

SwiftUI introduces a new way of thinking about user interfaces by allowing developers to focus on describing the *state* of their app, and not worrying about how to manually update the view hierarchy. This reduces boilerplate code and makes it easier to create responsive, dynamic interfaces that update as the data changes.

For example, a simple label in SwiftUI can be defined as:

```
Text("Hello, World!")
```

This line of code will display a label that automatically updates when the underlying state changes.

## Creating Views and Modifiers

SwiftUI is built on a rich set of **views** and **modifiers** that allow you to build flexible user interfaces. Views are the building blocks of the user interface, while modifiers allow you to customize their appearance and behavior.

### Basic Views

SwiftUI offers a wide variety of built-in views such as **Text**, **Image**, **Button**, and **List**. These views are highly customizable using modifiers.

```
Text("Hello, SwiftUI!")
    .font(.title)
    .foregroundColor(.blue)
```

### Modifiers

Modifiers allow you to apply transformations to views, such as changing colors, applying padding, or setting alignments. SwiftUI's modifier system is chainable, meaning you can stack multiple modifiers on a single view to adjust its appearance in a concise manner.

```
Image(systemName: "star.fill")
    .resizable()
    .frame(width: 50, height: 50)
    .foregroundColor(.yellow)
```

# State Management in SwiftUI: Observables, State, and Bindings

State management is a critical aspect of SwiftUI. Understanding how to use **State**, **Binding**, and **ObservableObject** allows developers to create dynamic apps that respond to user input and changes in data.

**State in SwiftUI**

The **@State** property wrapper is used to store local, mutable state in a view. When the state changes, SwiftUI automatically updates the UI to reflect the new value.

```
@State private var counter = 0

Button("Increment") {
    counter += 1
}
```

**Binding**

The **@Binding** property wrapper is used to create a two-way connection between a parent view and a child view. This allows changes in the child view's state to propagate back to the parent.

```
struct CounterView: View {
    @Binding var count: Int
    var body: some View {
        Button("Increment") {
            count += 1
        }
    }
}
```

**ObservableObject and EnvironmentObject**

The **@ObservableObject** property wrapper allows for the creation of model objects that are observed by SwiftUI views. When the model's data changes, the views observing that model are updated. **@EnvironmentObject** is used to share observable data across different views in the view hierarchy.

```swift
class UserData: ObservableObject {
    @Published var name = "John"
}


struct ProfileView: View {
    @EnvironmentObject var userData: UserData
    var body: some View {
        Text(userData.name)
    }
}
```

# Working with SwiftUI Previews and the Canvas

SwiftUI's **previews** are a powerful tool that allows developers to visualize their user interfaces as they work on them. By rendering a live preview of the view, developers can instantly see how the UI looks and behaves.

**Creating Previews**

To create a preview, you simply use the `PreviewProvider` protocol. The `preview` function inside this protocol allows you to define the view to be previewed.

```swift
struct ContentView_Previews: PreviewProvider {
    static var previews: some View {
        ContentView()
    }
}
```

**Real-Time UI Development with SwiftUI Previews**

One of the most significant advantages of SwiftUI is its ability to generate real-time previews that update as you write code. This allows you to experiment

with design and layout changes without having to manually build and run the app each time.

# Chapter 3

# Advanced Swift Programming for iOS

## Protocols, Generics, and Extensions: Unlocking Swift's Full Potential

Swift is a language that thrives on flexibility and power, which is evident through its extensive use of protocols, generics, and extensions. These features allow developers to write clean, reusable, and highly adaptable code. In this chapter, we will explore how these advanced concepts enable developers to unlock Swift's full potential, making applications more robust and maintainable.

### Protocols: Defining Blueprints for Behavior

Protocols in Swift define a blueprint for methods, properties, and other requirements that suit a particular task or piece of functionality. Classes, structs, or enums can then adopt these protocols, promising to implement the required methods and properties. This enables Swift to be more flexible and modular, ensuring that different types can conform to the same protocol, making code more scalable.

For example, a simple protocol might look like this:

```
protocol Drivable {
    func startEngine()
    func stopEngine()
}
```

A class that conforms to the `Drivable` protocol must implement both `startEngine()` and `stopEngine()`:

```
class Car: Drivable {
    func startEngine() {
        print("Car engine started.")
    }

    func stopEngine() {
        print("Car engine stopped.")
    }
}
```

Protocols provide powerful tools for abstraction and can be extended to provide default implementations, which significantly reduces boilerplate code.

**Generics: Writing Flexible and Reusable Code**

Generics are one of the most powerful features in Swift. They allow you to write flexible, reusable functions, classes, and data structures without sacrificing type safety. Generics enable you to create methods and data types that can work with any type, subject to the constraints you define.

For example, a generic function for swapping two values might look like this:

```
func swapValues<T>(_ a: inout T, _ b: inout T) {
    let temp = a
    a = b
    b = temp
}

var x = 5
var y = 10
swapValues(&x, &y)  // x is now 10, y is now 5
```

The T represents a placeholder for a specific type, allowing the `swapValues` function to work with any data type that is provided to it. This makes generics an excellent tool for creating flexible and reusable code, especially when working with collections or algorithms.

**Extensions: Enhancing Existing Types**

Extensions allow developers to add new functionality to existing classes, structs, or enums without modifying the original source code. This is particularly useful when working with system libraries or when you need to customize the behavior of third-party code.

```
extension String {
    func reversedString() -> String {
        return String(self.reversed())
    }
}

let original = "Swift"
print(original.reversedString())  // Output: tfiwS
```

Extensions are also useful for adhering to protocols. You can extend a type to conform to a protocol without changing its original implementation, which is perfect for adding behavior to existing types without touching their internals.

# Mastering Protocol-Oriented Programming

Protocol-Oriented Programming (POP) is a paradigm that prioritizes protocols over inheritance, focusing on behavior rather than class hierarchies. Swift's protocol-oriented approach to programming introduces a paradigm shift where protocols, not classes or structs, are the central building blocks of your code.

**Why Use Protocol-Oriented Programming?**

POP emphasizes flexibility and code reuse. Unlike traditional object-oriented programming, which relies heavily on inheritance, POP encourages composing behavior through protocols. This leads to more maintainable and extensible code since protocols define behavior that can be shared across different types, making code more modular and adaptable.

For example, you can use protocol extensions to provide default implementations, significantly reducing the amount of boilerplate code needed in your classes.

```swift
protocol Flyable {
    func fly()
}

extension Flyable {
    func fly() {
        print("Flying in the sky!")
    }
}

struct Bird: Flyable {}

let bird = Bird()
bird.fly()  // Output: Flying in the sky!
```

In this example, we can see that the `Flyable` protocol provides a default implementation of the `fly()` method. Types that conform to `Flyable` automatically gain this behavior, enabling code reuse without the need for subclassing.

**Protocol Composition and Multiple Inheritance**

Swift allows you to compose multiple protocols into a single requirement, which means that you can mix and match various behaviors into one type. This allows you to simulate multiple inheritance, something that is typically not possible in traditional object-oriented programming.

```swift
protocol Swimmer {
    func swim()
}

protocol Runner {
    func run()
}

struct Athlete: Swimmer, Runner {
    func swim() {
        print("Swimming!")
    }

    func run() {
        print("Running!")
    }
}

let athlete = Athlete()
athlete.swim()  // Output: Swimming!
athlete.run()   // Output: Running!
```

Here, the `Athlete` struct conforms to both `Swimmer` and `Runner`, combining both behaviors. This is an effective way to build highly modular and adaptable code using protocols.

## Using Generics to Build Flexible and Reusable Code

Generics provide a mechanism for writing code that works with any type while preserving type safety. By abstracting types, you can build reusable algorithms, collections, and structures. Swift's generics allow you to create flexible APIs that can be used with various types.

**Generic Functions**

A generic function can operate on any type, as shown in the earlier example with `swapValues`. This makes your code more reusable without losing the advantages of type safety.

**Generic Data Structures**

Generics are also beneficial for building data structures like arrays, stacks, and queues that work with any type of data. For instance, here's a simple implementation of a generic stack:

```swift
struct Stack<T> {
   var items: [T] = []

   mutating func push(_ item: T) {
      items.append(item)
   }

   mutating func pop() -> T? {
      return items.popLast()
   }
}


var intStack = Stack<Int>()
intStack.push(10)
intStack.push(20)
print(intStack.pop())  // Output: Optional(20)
```

In this example, the `Stack` struct can store any type of data, providing flexibility while maintaining type safety.

## Concurrency and Multithreading in Swift

Concurrency and multithreading are critical when building performance-sensitive iOS applications. Swift offers several tools to manage concurrency, allowing developers to execute tasks in parallel and improve app responsiveness.

## Concurrency with Grand Central Dispatch (GCD)

GCD is a powerful tool for managing concurrent tasks in Swift. It allows developers to dispatch tasks asynchronously or synchronously to different queues. This is particularly useful for handling tasks that would otherwise block the main thread, such as network requests or file operations.

```swift
DispatchQueue.global(qos: .background).async {
    // Perform heavy work in the background
    print("Background work done")
}
```

```swift
DispatchQueue.main.async {
    // Update UI on the main thread
    print("UI updated")
}
```

In the example above, we use GCD to execute a background task asynchronously and then return to the main thread to update the user interface.

## Swift Concurrency: Async/Await

With Swift's new concurrency model, introduced in Swift 5.5, the `async` and `await` keywords provide a simpler and more readable way to handle asynchronous operations. By marking a function with `async`, you indicate that it can be suspended and resumed later, making the code easier to understand and manage.

```swift
func fetchData() async -> String {
    let data = await networkRequest()
    return data
}
```

The `await` keyword tells Swift to pause the function's execution until the asynchronous task completes, significantly simplifying asynchronous programming.

### Error Handling in Concurrency

Concurrency introduces challenges in handling errors, as errors may occur on different threads. Swift provides robust error-handling mechanisms through the use of `do`, `try`, and `catch` blocks. When working with asynchronous code, errors can be thrown and caught using `try` in an `async` function.

```swift
func fetchData() async throws -> String {
    let data = try await networkRequest()
    return data
}
```

## Error Handling and Debugging Advanced Swift Code

As your Swift code grows in complexity, managing errors and debugging becomes even more critical. Swift provides robust tools for handling errors and debugging, ensuring that you can quickly identify and fix issues.

### Best Practices for Error Handling

Error handling in Swift revolves around the `Error` protocol and the use of `do-catch` blocks. It's essential to handle errors gracefully, especially when working with asynchronous code or external resources like APIs.

A best practice is to always handle errors explicitly and avoid relying on the default `fatalError()` or `assertionFailure()` for recoverable errors. Instead, throw and catch errors, and provide meaningful error messages or recovery actions to enhance the user experience.

```swift
enum NetworkError: Error {
    case noInternet
```

```
    case serverDown
}

func fetchData() throws {
    // Simulate network failure
    throw NetworkError.noInternet
}
```

**Leveraging Debugging Tools for Complex Issues**

Xcode provides a powerful set of debugging tools that allow you to set breakpoints, inspect variables, and trace program execution step by step. Key tools include:

- **LLDB**: The debugger for inspecting and manipulating Swift objects and variables during runtime.

- **Instruments**: A tool for profiling and analyzing the performance of your app, detecting memory leaks, and identifying bottlenecks.

- **Console Output**: The debug console provides insights into runtime issues, allowing you to print values and track function calls during app execution.

By using these tools, you can easily track down and resolve issues in your advanced Swift code, ensuring your app runs efficiently and reliably.

# Chapter 4

# Deep Dive into SwiftUI Views and Layouts

## Understanding SwiftUI Views: From Simple to Complex

SwiftUI revolutionizes the way developers create user interfaces by providing a declarative syntax that makes building complex interfaces simpler and more intuitive. The foundation of SwiftUI lies in its **views**, which represent the visual components of an application. From basic UI elements like text and images to more complex, customizable components, SwiftUI offers a vast range of tools for creating user interfaces efficiently.

### Basic SwiftUI Views: Building Blocks of Your Interface

At the simplest level, SwiftUI includes fundamental views such as `Text`, `Image`, `Button`, and `VStack`. These elements can be easily manipulated and customized to create dynamic user interfaces.

```
Text("Hello, SwiftUI!")
   .font(.title)
   .foregroundColor(.blue)


Image(systemName: "star.fill")
   .resizable()
   .scaledToFit()
   .frame(width: 50, height: 50)
```

With just a few lines of code, you can display text and images with styling applied. SwiftUI's declarative nature allows you to modify properties in a straightforward manner, making these views incredibly flexible.

**Creating Custom Views**

While standard views are powerful, SwiftUI's true strength lies in its ability to create custom views that can be reused throughout an application. You can encapsulate complex UI logic within custom views, making your code more modular and reusable.

```
struct CustomButton: View {
    var title: String
    var action: () -> Void

    var body: some View {
        Button(action: action) {
            Text(title)
                .font(.headline)
                .padding()
                .background(Color.blue)
                .foregroundColor(.white)
                .cornerRadius(10)
        }
    }
}
```

In this example, we define a reusable `CustomButton` view that accepts a title and an action. This custom view can be used throughout your application wherever you need a button, promoting consistency and reducing code duplication.

## Stacks, Grids, and Lists: Advanced Layout Techniques

SwiftUI introduces a number of layout components that simplify the process of arranging views in a structured way. **Stacks**, **Grids**, and **Lists** are powerful tools that allow developers to create highly flexible layouts with minimal code.

**Using Stacks for Vertical and Horizontal Layouts**

Stacks are the building blocks of layout management in SwiftUI. You can use `VStack` to arrange views vertically and `HStack` to arrange views horizontally. These containers manage the layout of their child views automatically, adjusting based on the content they hold.

```
VStack {
    Text("Welcome to SwiftUI")
    Text("Let's learn more!")
}
```

The `VStack` will automatically place the texts one on top of the other, making the code both simple and declarative. Similarly, `HStack` arranges views horizontally.

**Grids for Advanced Layouts**

For more complex layouts, **LazyVGrid** and **LazyHGrid** are useful for organizing views in a grid format. These grids allow for more control over the positioning and spacing of elements, and they can handle dynamic content efficiently.

```
let columns = [
    GridItem(.flexible()),
    GridItem(.flexible())
]

LazyVGrid(columns: columns) {
    ForEach(1..<6) { index in
        Text("Item \(index)")
            .frame(width: 100, height: 100)
            .background(Color.blue)
            .cornerRadius(10)
```

```
    }
}
```

This creates a flexible grid where each cell adapts to the content, making it ideal for displaying dynamic lists or images in a grid-like fashion.

**Creating Dynamic Lists with SwiftUI**

**List** is another powerful view that allows you to display dynamic content in a scrollable list format. Whether it's a simple list of strings or a complex collection of data models, SwiftUI handles it effortlessly.

```
List(0..<10) { number in
    Text("Item \(number)")
}
```

SwiftUI's `List` automatically handles things like scroll management, item reordering, and cell recycling, making it ideal for creating lists with a large number of elements. You can also customize each cell with complex views or data models.

# Responsive UI Design with SwiftUI

SwiftUI excels at creating **responsive UIs**, which automatically adapt to different screen sizes and orientations. The declarative syntax makes it easy to design layouts that look great on devices with varying screen sizes, such as iPhones, iPads, and Macs.

**Using GeometryReader for Dynamic Layouts**

`GeometryReader` is a powerful tool that allows you to build layouts that adapt based on the available space. It gives you access to the size and position of views within their parent containers, allowing for more dynamic and responsive designs.

```
GeometryReader { geometry in
    Text("Width: \(geometry.size.width), Height: \(geometry.size.height)")
```

```
}
```

You can use `GeometryReader` to adjust the layout based on the screen size or orientation, ensuring that your UI adapts to different environments seamlessly.

**Conditional Layouts with `@Environment`**

SwiftUI provides the `@Environment` property wrapper, which allows you to access environment values like device orientation or screen size. This lets you adjust your layouts based on these values.

```
@Environment(\.horizontalSizeClass) var sizeClass
```

```
var body: some View {
    if sizeClass == .compact {
        Text("Compact View")
    } else {
        Text("Regular View")
    }
}
```

This allows you to create adaptive user interfaces that respond to the environment in real-time, providing users with a better experience across multiple devices.

## Creating Adaptive Interfaces for iPhone, iPad, and Mac

Building apps for multiple platforms often involves creating adaptive interfaces that adjust to the specific needs of each device. SwiftUI makes it easy to create interfaces that behave differently on iPhones, iPads, and Macs.

**Platform-Specific Views with `@ViewBuilder`**

SwiftUI's `@ViewBuilder` allows developers to create conditional views based on the target platform. This means you can customize the UI for iPhone, iPad, or Mac without writing platform-specific code elsewhere in your app.

```
@ViewBuilder var platformSpecificView: some View {
    if UIDevice.current.userInterfaceIdiom == .phone {
        Text("This is an iPhone")
    } else if UIDevice.current.userInterfaceIdiom == .pad {
        Text("This is an iPad")
    } else {
        Text("This is a Mac")
    }
}
```

This approach ensures your UI is optimized for the specific platform while maintaining a single codebase.

### Creating Multi-Window Layouts for iPad and Mac

On iPad and Mac, users can run apps in multiple windows. SwiftUI provides a mechanism to manage these multiple windows and adapt your layout accordingly. The `WindowGroup` view allows for the management of multiple windows within the same app.

```
WindowGroup {
    ContentView()
}
```

This simple construct allows you to design your app's behavior and layout in response to multi-window environments, a feature especially useful on iPadOS and macOS.

## Handling Different Screen Sizes and Orientations

With iOS devices available in various screen sizes and orientations, handling these differences in your layout is crucial for providing a consistent user experience. SwiftUI simplifies this with adaptive layout tools.

**Auto Layout with SwiftUI**

SwiftUI automatically applies layout constraints based on the parent view's size, ensuring that elements resize or reposition themselves depending on the screen size and orientation. However, for more granular control, you can also use modifiers like `.frame()`, `.padding()`, and `.alignmentGuide()` to manually adjust how elements appear on different screen sizes.

```
Text("Hello, World!")
   .frame(width: 300, height: 200)
   .padding()
   .background(Color.blue)
```

These tools enable you to design flexible, responsive interfaces that behave correctly regardless of the device's size or orientation.

## Animations in SwiftUI: Creating Fluid User Experiences

Animations are a key part of providing a smooth and engaging user experience in modern apps. SwiftUI simplifies animation with built-in support for both **implicit** and **explicit** animations, allowing you to animate views with ease.

### Implicit Animations: Quick and Simple

Implicit animations are those that are automatically triggered when a property change occurs. With SwiftUI, you can apply animations to state changes, making UI updates fluid and natural.

```
@State private var isTapped = false

var body: some View {
   Button(action: {
```

```
    withAnimation {
       isTapped.toggle()
    }
  }) {
    Circle()
       .frame(width: 100, height: 100)
       .foregroundColor(isTapped ? .red : .blue)
    }
}
```

In this example, the circle's color changes with an implicit animation when the button is tapped, creating a smooth transition between states.

**Explicit Animations: Fine-Tuned Control**

For more precise control over animations, SwiftUI offers explicit animations. You can specify which properties should animate and control the duration, timing curve, and delay.

```
withAnimation(.easeIn(duration: 2.0)) {
    isTapped.toggle()
}
```

Explicit animations provide more control, allowing for complex animations like rotations, scaling, or transforming views based on user interaction or other triggers.

## Advanced Transition and Gesture Handling

SwiftUI allows developers to implement advanced gestures and transitions to create more dynamic interactions. These features enable the development of intuitive and responsive interfaces that react to user input seamlessly.

**Custom Transitions**

SwiftUI provides a variety of built-in transitions, such as `.slide`, `.move`, and `.opacity`, but you can also create custom transitions for more complex animations.

```
Text("Welcome!")
    .transition(.slide)
```

This transition causes the view to slide in or out of the screen. Custom transitions can also involve combining different animation effects for unique interactions.

**Gesture Handling: Interactivity in Your App**

SwiftUI makes it easy to add gesture recognizers to views, enabling users to interact with your app through taps, swipes, pinches, and more. For example, you can use a `DragGesture` to let users drag views around.

```
@State private var offset = CGSize.zero

var body: some View {
    Text("Drag Me!")
        .padding()
        .background(Color.blue)
        .cornerRadius(10)
        .offset(offset)
        .gesture(
            DragGesture()
                .onChanged { value in
                    offset = value.translation
                }
                .onEnded { _ in
                    offset = .zero
                }
        )
}
```

Gestures enhance the interactivity of your application, allowing you to create fluid, touch-responsive user experiences.

# Chapter 5

# Data Management with SwiftUI

## Binding Data: How to Work with SwiftUI's State System

In SwiftUI, data management is a critical aspect of building dynamic and interactive applications. SwiftUI's declarative nature allows for efficient state management, providing a streamlined way to bind data to the user interface. One of the most powerful features in SwiftUI is the state system, which allows you to manage and update the view hierarchy based on changes in your data.

### What is Data Binding in SwiftUI?

Data binding in SwiftUI refers to the process of connecting a view to some underlying data. When the data changes, the view automatically updates to reflect those changes, creating a seamless and interactive user experience. The state system is essential for maintaining this connection between data and the UI.

To bind data in SwiftUI, you can use the `@State`, `@Binding`, and `@Environment` property wrappers. Each of these plays a distinct role in managing and passing data throughout your views.

### Understanding @State, @Binding, and @Environment

- **@State:** The `@State` property wrapper is used to manage local, view-specific data. When you use `@State`, SwiftUI automatically tracks changes to that data and updates the view accordingly. It's ideal for data that doesn't need to be shared with other views.

```
@State private var isToggled = false

var body: some View {
    Toggle("Enable Feature", isOn: $isToggled)
}
```

In this example, the state of the toggle is stored locally within the view. Any change in the toggle automatically updates the UI.

- **@Binding:** The `@Binding` property wrapper is used to pass state data between parent and child views. It allows a child view to modify the state managed by a parent view, creating a one-way data flow.

```
struct ToggleSwitch: View {
    @Binding var isOn: Bool

    var body: some View {
        Toggle("Enable Feature", isOn: $isOn)
    }
}
```

```
struct ContentView: View {
    @State private var isFeatureEnabled = false

    var body: some View {
        ToggleSwitch(isOn: $isFeatureEnabled)
    }
}
```

Here, `@Binding` creates a two-way connection between the parent (`ContentView`) and the child (`ToggleSwitch`) views, allowing changes in one to automatically propagate to the other.

- **@Environment:** The `@Environment` property wrapper is used to pass data from a higher-level environment to any child view within the same view hierarchy. It's ideal for managing app-wide settings like color schemes, localization, or user preferences.

@Environment(\.colorScheme) var colorScheme

var body: some View {
   Text("Current mode: \(colorScheme == .dark ? "Dark" : "Light")")
}

This example demonstrates how `@Environment` can be used to retrieve global app settings, like the current color scheme.

**Advanced State Management Patterns**

As your application grows in complexity, managing state can become increasingly difficult. SwiftUI provides several advanced state management patterns to help handle more intricate scenarios.

- **ObservableObject and @Published:** For more complex data models, you can use the `@ObservableObject` protocol, which allows for sharing state across multiple views. The `@Published` property wrapper is used to automatically trigger UI updates when a property changes.

class UserData: ObservableObject {
   @Published var username: String = "Guest"
}

By using `@ObservableObject`, you can bind multiple views to the same data model, making it easier to keep all relevant views in sync.

- **EnvironmentObject:** For global data that needs to be accessed throughout the app, you can use the `@EnvironmentObject` property wrapper. This allows you to inject an object into the environment, making it accessible in any view in the hierarchy.

```
class AppData: ObservableObject {
  @Published var userLoggedIn = false
}

@main
struct MyApp: App {
  var appData = AppData()

  var body: some Scene {
    WindowGroup {
      ContentView()
          .environmentObject(appData)
    }
  }
}
```

In this example, the `AppData` object is made available to all views in the app, ensuring consistent data access across the application.

## Handling User Input with SwiftUI Forms and Controls

SwiftUI makes it easy to create forms and controls for handling user input. Whether you're collecting basic text information or more complex data like dates and selections, SwiftUI provides a range of tools for building interactive forms.

### Creating Forms for User Input

The `Form` view in SwiftUI is a container that groups together various input elements. Forms are commonly used for settings pages, sign-ups, and other scenarios where the user is required to input data.

```
Form {
    TextField("Enter your name", text: $name)
    DatePicker("Select a date", selection: $date)
    Picker("Choose an option", selection: $selectedOption) {
        Text("Option 1").tag(1)
        Text("Option 2").tag(2)
    }
}
```

In this form, we have a `TextField`, `DatePicker`, and `Picker`, all of which are bound to the view's state. Any changes to these controls automatically update the bound data.

**Validating User Input**

Validation is an essential aspect of handling user input. SwiftUI provides tools for adding validation to forms, ensuring that the data entered by the user meets specific criteria.

```
TextField("Enter email", text: $email)
    .keyboardType(.emailAddress)
    .onChange(of: email) { newValue in
        isValidEmail = newValue.isValidEmail() // Custom email validation
    }
```

In this example, a custom validation method (`isValidEmail()`) is called whenever the email text field changes, ensuring the input meets the required format.

**Building Dynamic Forms and Interactive Interfaces**

SwiftUI makes it easy to build dynamic forms that adapt based on user input. You can show or hide form elements, enable or disable controls, and change the layout of your form based on specific conditions.

```
if showAdvancedOptions {
    Toggle("Enable Advanced Settings", isOn: $isAdvancedEnabled)
    TextField("Additional Notes", text: $notes)
}
```

By using state to control the visibility of different sections, you can create interactive forms that respond dynamically to user choices.

## Core Data and SwiftUI: Integrating Local Storage

Local data storage is often an essential part of mobile applications. Core Data is Apple's framework for managing persistent data, and with SwiftUI, integrating Core Data into your app has become much easier.

### Setting Up Core Data in a SwiftUI App

To use Core Data in a SwiftUI app, you first need to create a `PersistenceController` that sets up the Core Data stack. This is typically done in the app's entry point.

```
class PersistenceController {
    static let shared = PersistenceController()

    let container: NSPersistentContainer

    init() {
        container = NSPersistentContainer(name: "MyApp")
        container.loadPersistentStores { (description, error) in
            if let error = error {
                fatalError("Unresolved error \(error)")
            }
```

```
        }
    }
}
```

This code sets up the Core Data stack with a persistent container that handles data saving and retrieval.

**Fetching and Displaying Core Data Objects**

Once the Core Data stack is set up, you can fetch data using `@FetchRequest` in SwiftUI views. This allows you to display Core Data objects directly in your UI.

```
struct ContentView: View {
    @FetchRequest(sortDescriptors: [SortDescriptor(\.name)]) var items:
FetchedResults<Item>

    var body: some View {
        List(items) { item in
            Text(item.name ?? "Unnamed")
        }
    }
}
```

In this example, `@FetchRequest` is used to automatically fetch and display `Item` objects from Core Data. The fetched data is automatically updated when changes are made.

**Adding, Updating, and Deleting Data with Core Data**

To manage the data in Core Data, you need to be able to add, update, and delete objects. SwiftUI's data bindings make this process intuitive.

**Adding Data**

```
let newItem = Item(context: viewContext)
newItem.name = "New Item"
```

```
try? viewContext.save()
```

This code creates a new `Item` object, sets its properties, and saves it to the persistent store.

**Updating Data**

```
if let item = items.first {
    item.name = "Updated Item"
    try? viewContext.save()
}
```

Here, we modify the first item in the fetched results and save the updated data.

**Deleting Data**

```
if let itemToDelete = items.first {
    viewContext.delete(itemToDelete)
    try? viewContext.save()
}
```

To delete an object, you simply call `delete()` on the managed object context and then save the changes.

## Advanced Core Data Integration in SwiftUI Apps

For larger apps with more complex data models, you may need to integrate advanced Core Data techniques, such as background context management, efficient fetching, and handling large data sets.

**Using Background Contexts**

When performing heavy data operations, such as fetching or saving large datasets, it's best to use background contexts to avoid blocking the main UI thread.

```
let backgroundContext =
PersistenceController.shared.container.newBackgroundContext()
backgroundContext.perform {
    // Perform data operations on the background context
}
```

### Efficient Fetching

When working with large datasets, it's important to fetch only the data you need. Core Data allows you to perform efficient queries using predicates and sorting.

```
@FetchRequest(fetchRequest: Item.fetchRequest())
var items: FetchedResults<Item>
```

By optimizing your fetch requests, you can ensure that your app

performs efficiently even with large datasets.

## Fetching, Updating, and Deleting Data Efficiently

Efficiently managing data in SwiftUI apps is key to providing a smooth user experience. The use of Core Data, combined with SwiftUI's state system, allows you to efficiently manage and update data across your views.

By leveraging tools such as background contexts and efficient fetch requests, you can ensure that your app performs optimally while maintaining an interactive and dynamic user interface.

# Chapter 6

# Networking and API Integration

Networking and API integration are essential parts of modern app development. Whether you're building a data-driven app that fetches information from an online service or creating a real-time application that communicates continuously with a backend, understanding how to handle networking efficiently is critical. In Swift, there are several powerful tools and frameworks to work with APIs, manage real-time data, and ensure security. This chapter will explore the fundamental techniques and best practices for working with APIs and networking in Swift, including handling data fetching, error management, real-time communication, and secure requests.

## Working with REST APIs in Swift

REST (Representational State Transfer) APIs are one of the most common methods for exchanging data between a client and a server. Swift provides several tools to help you easily integrate and interact with REST APIs.

### Making Network Requests with URLSession

The `URLSession` class is a powerful tool in Swift that allows you to send HTTP requests and receive responses from a server. It supports various types of requests, including GET, POST, PUT, and DELETE.

Here is an example of how you can make a simple GET request to fetch data from a REST API:

import Foundation

```
let url = URL(string: "https://api.example.com/data")!
let task = URLSession.shared.dataTask(with: url) { data, response, error in
    if let error = error {
        print("Error: \(error.localizedDescription)")
        return
    }

    guard let data = data else {
        print("No data received")
        return
    }

    // Handle the data (e.g., decode it into a model)
}
task.resume()
```

In this example, a request is made to a URL, and the server's response is handled asynchronously. You can process the data or handle errors within the closure.

**Sending POST Requests**

To send data to a server, such as when submitting a form or updating data, you use a POST request. Here's an example of sending JSON data:

```
import Foundation

let url = URL(string: "https://api.example.com/submit")!
var request = URLRequest(url: url)
request.httpMethod = "POST"
request.setValue("application/json", forHTTPHeaderField: "Content-Type")

let body: [String: Any] = ["name": "John", "age": 30]
request.httpBody = try? JSONSerialization.data(withJSONObject: body)
```

```
let task = URLSession.shared.dataTask(with: request) { data, response, error in
    if let error = error {
        print("Error: \(error.localizedDescription)")
        return
    }

    guard let data = data else {
        print("No data received")
        return
    }

    // Handle the response
}
task.resume()
```

In this case, the data is encoded into JSON format and sent as part of the HTTP body.

## Fetching and Decoding Data with Swift

One of the key aspects of working with APIs is decoding the data into usable models. Swift offers the `Codable` protocol, which allows you to easily parse JSON data into native Swift types.

### Using Codable to Parse JSON

Consider an example where you are fetching a list of users from an API. You would define a model that conforms to `Codable`:

```
struct User: Codable {
    let id: Int
    let name: String
    let email: String
}
```

```swift
let url = URL(string: "https://api.example.com/users")!
let task = URLSession.shared.dataTask(with: url) { data, response, error in
    if let error = error {
        print("Error: \(error.localizedDescription)")
        return
    }

    guard let data = data else {
        print("No data received")
        return
    }

    do {
        let decoder = JSONDecoder()
        let users = try decoder.decode([User].self, from: data)
        // Use the users array
    } catch {
        print("Decoding error: \(error.localizedDescription)")
    }
}
task.resume()
```

In this example, the JSON response is decoded into an array of `User` objects. Swift's `JSONDecoder` automatically maps the JSON data to the struct's properties.

**Error Handling During Decoding**

When working with APIs, errors can arise in many areas, including during decoding. Swift provides a robust way to handle these errors using `do-catch` blocks, ensuring that your app doesn't crash unexpectedly.

```swift
do {
    let users = try decoder.decode([User].self, from: data)
} catch let decodingError {
```

```
print("Decoding error: \(decodingError.localizedDescription)")
}
```

This ensures that if the response data cannot be decoded properly (e.g., if the structure doesn't match the expected model), your app can handle the error gracefully.

# Error Handling in Networking Operations

Error handling is a crucial part of networking, especially when dealing with unreliable or slow network conditions. Swift provides several mechanisms to help you manage errors that may occur during network requests.

### Common Network Errors

When using `URLSession`, network errors can occur for several reasons, such as timeouts, connection failures, or server errors. These errors are typically passed as an `Error` object in the completion handler. Common error types include:

- `URLError`: Represents network-related errors such as timeout or unreachable network.

- `HTTPURLResponse`: Provides HTTP status codes that indicate the success or failure of the request.

```
if let error = error {
    print("Network error: \(error.localizedDescription)")
    return
}
```

```
if let response = response as? HTTPURLResponse, response.statusCode != 200 {
    print("Server error: Status code \(response.statusCode)")
    return
}
```

In this example, we check for both network errors and HTTP status codes, handling each case appropriately.

**Retrying Failed Requests**

Sometimes, network requests fail due to temporary conditions (e.g., weak connection). Implementing retry logic can improve user experience. You can retry a failed request a specific number of times before giving up.

```swift
func fetchData(attempt: Int = 1) {
    let maxAttempts = 3
    let url = URL(string: "https://api.example.com/data")!

    let task = URLSession.shared.dataTask(with: url) { data, response, error in
        if let error = error {
            if attempt < maxAttempts {
                fetchData(attempt: attempt + 1)
            } else {
                print("Final attempt failed: \(error.localizedDescription)")
            }
            return
        }

        // Handle successful response
    }
    task.resume()
}
```

This function retries the request up to three times if it encounters a failure.

# Real-Time Networking: WebSockets and Combine

Real-time applications, such as chat apps or live notifications, often require continuous data communication with the server. WebSockets and the Combine framework offer powerful solutions for real-time networking in Swift.

**Building Real-Time Applications with WebSockets**

WebSockets provide a full-duplex communication channel over a single, long-lived connection, making them ideal for real-time applications. In Swift, you can use libraries like `URLSessionWebSocketTask` to handle WebSocket connections.

```swift
let url = URL(string: "wss://api.example.com/socket")!
let webSocketTask = URLSession.shared.webSocketTask(with: url)

webSocketTask.resume()

// Sending a message
let message = URLSessionWebSocketTask.Message.string("Hello, server!")
webSocketTask.send(message) { error in
    if let error = error {
        print("Error sending message: \(error.localizedDescription)")
    }
}

// Receiving messages
webSocketTask.receive { result in
    switch result {
    case .success(let message):
        switch message {
        case .string(let text):
            print("Received message: \(text)")
        default:
            break
        }
    case .failure(let error):
        print("Error receiving message: \(error.localizedDescription)")
    }
```

```
}
```

This example shows how to set up a WebSocket connection, send messages, and receive updates from the server.

**Reactive Programming with Combine**

Combine is a declarative framework for processing values over time. It can be used for handling asynchronous events like network responses, making it an excellent fit for real-time networking.

You can use Combine's `URLSession.DataTaskPublisher` to handle network requests reactively:

```
import Combine

let url = URL(string: "https://api.example.com/data")!
let publisher = URLSession.shared.dataTaskPublisher(for: url)
    .map { data, response in
        // Process the data here
        return data
    }
    .catch { error in
        Just(Data()) // Return an empty data object on error
    }
    .sink { data in
        // Handle the fetched data
    }
```

With Combine, you can chain operators to transform data, handle errors, and manage asynchronous tasks.

# Secure Networking and Best Practices

When working with networking, ensuring data security is paramount. This section covers essential practices to keep your network requests secure.

**Handling Authentication**

Many APIs require authentication, often through tokens like OAuth or API keys. Securely storing and using these tokens is crucial.

You can store sensitive data, like authentication tokens, in the iOS keychain:

```
import Security

// Example: Storing an API token in the Keychain
func saveApiToken(_ token: String) {
    let query: [CFString: Any] = [
        kSecClass: kSecClassGenericPassword,
        kSecAttrAccount: "apiToken",
        kSecValueData: token.data(using: .utf8)!
    ]

    SecItemAdd(query as CFDictionary, nil)
}
```

This code stores the API token securely in the keychain, ensuring that it is not exposed in plain text.

**OAuth and HTTPS Requests**

OAuth is commonly used for secure authorization, especially when interacting with third-party services. When making API requests with OAuth, you need to include the access token in the request header.

```
var request = URLRequest(url: URL(string: "https://api.example.com/data")!)
request.setValue("Bearer \(accessToken)", forHTTPHeaderField: "Authorization")
```

This code adds the OAuth token to the `Authorization` header, allowing you to authenticate API requests securely.

**HTTPS Requests**

Always use HTTPS for secure communication between your app and the server. HTTPS encrypts data in transit, protecting it from interception.

```
let

url = URL(string: "https://api.example.com/data")!
```

By using `https://`, you ensure that all data sent between your app and the server is encrypted.

# Chapter 7

# Advanced SwiftUI Components and Patterns

In SwiftUI, the flexibility and power of its components make it a compelling framework for building visually rich and interactive applications. As you progress from basic layouts to more complex and dynamic UIs, understanding advanced SwiftUI components and patterns becomes essential. This chapter explores the creation of custom views, reusable components, the use of view modifiers, managing large data-driven views, and crafting intricate animations and transitions. These skills will allow you to design scalable, maintainable, and visually engaging applications.

## Creating Custom Views and Reusable Components

One of the core strengths of SwiftUI is the ability to create custom views that can be reused across your application. Custom views allow for modularity and maintainability, as they encapsulate UI logic in a way that promotes reusability.

### Defining Custom Views

Custom views are created by structuring them as SwiftUI `View` structs. Each custom view can accept parameters to customize its appearance and behavior. For example, a simple custom button might look like this:

```
struct CustomButton: View {
    var title: String
    var action: () -> Void
```

```
var body: some View {
    Button(action: action) {
        Text(title)
            .font(.headline)
            .padding()
            .background(Color.blue)
            .foregroundColor(.white)
            .cornerRadius(10)
    }
  }
}
```

This `CustomButton` view accepts a `title` and an `action` closure, making it reusable throughout the app. The body defines its appearance using standard SwiftUI components like `Button`, `Text`, and modifiers such as `padding()`, `background()`, and `cornerRadius()`.

**Customizing Views with Parameters**

In addition to static properties like `title`, custom views can accept a wide variety of parameters to control aspects like color, size, layout, and even behavior. The flexibility allows you to create views that fit your app's specific needs without needing to replicate code.

```
struct CustomCardView: View {
    var title: String
    var subtitle: String
    var backgroundColor: Color

    var body: some View {
        VStack {
            Text(title)
                .font(.title)
```

```
        .bold()
    Text(subtitle)
        .font(.subheadline)
        .foregroundColor(.gray)
    }
    .padding()
    .background(backgroundColor)
    .cornerRadius(12)
    .shadow(radius: 5)
    }
}
```

This `CustomCardView` accepts different strings for `title` and `subtitle`, as well as a customizable `backgroundColor`. By modifying the parameters, you can reuse this view for different sections of your app.

## Modularizing SwiftUI Code for Scalability

As apps grow in complexity, the ability to organize code into smaller, reusable components becomes essential. Modularizing your SwiftUI code ensures that your app remains manageable, scalable, and easy to update.

### Breaking Views into Subviews

A major way to modularize SwiftUI code is by breaking complex views into smaller subviews. Each subview encapsulates a piece of functionality, making the entire application easier to maintain and extend.

For instance, a large `ProfileView` might contain subviews for the user's profile picture, name, and bio. Instead of writing the layout directly in `ProfileView`, you can create smaller components for each:

```
struct ProfilePicture: View {
    var image: Image
```

```
    var body: some View {
      image
        .resizable()
        .scaledToFill()
        .clipShape(Circle())
        .frame(width: 100, height: 100)
    }
}

struct UserProfile: View {
  var name: String
  var bio: String

  var body: some View {
    VStack {
      Text(name)
        .font(.title)
        .bold()
      Text(bio)
        .font(.body)
        .foregroundColor(.gray)
    }
    .padding()
  }
}
```

This approach keeps the main `ProfileView` simpler and more focused, improving both readability and reusability.

## Using View Modifiers to Reuse Code

View modifiers are a powerful tool for reusing common styling or behavior in SwiftUI. By defining reusable view modifiers, you can easily apply consistent styling across multiple views without repeating code.

**Creating Custom View Modifiers**

Custom view modifiers allow you to encapsulate style and behavior in a reusable manner. A custom modifier can be applied to any view, making it easy to maintain a consistent look across your app.

For example, a `CardStyle` modifier might look like this:

```swift
struct CardStyle: ViewModifier {
    var backgroundColor: Color = .white
    var cornerRadius: CGFloat = 10
    var shadowRadius: CGFloat = 5

    func body(content: Content) -> some View {
        content
            .padding()
            .background(backgroundColor)
            .cornerRadius(cornerRadius)
            .shadow(radius: shadowRadius)
    }
}

extension View {
    func cardStyle(backgroundColor: Color = .white) -> some View {
        self.modifier(CardStyle(backgroundColor: backgroundColor))
    }
}
```

This custom modifier is now available for use across your app:

```swift
Text("Hello, World!")
    .cardStyle(backgroundColor: .blue)
```

By using view modifiers, you can easily apply complex styling logic to any view while keeping your codebase clean and manageable.

# Dynamic Lists and Collections in SwiftUI

SwiftUI makes it easy to build dynamic, scrollable lists and collections. Lists are a key feature in most apps, whether displaying a collection of items, user data, or feed content.

### Building Simple Lists

The `List` view in SwiftUI is a fundamental component for creating scrollable collections. It can display a simple static list or be dynamically populated with data.

Here's an example of a basic list displaying a collection of strings:

```
struct ItemListView: View {
    let items = ["Apple", "Banana", "Cherry"]

    var body: some View {
        List(items, id: \.self) { item in
            Text(item)
        }
    }
}
```

### Customizing List Rows

Each row in a `List` can be customized to display more complex content. For example, a list of users might include a profile picture, name, and status message:

```
struct User {
    var name: String
    var status: String
}

struct UserListView: View {
    let users = [
```

```
            User(name: "John Doe", status: "Online"),
            User(name: "Jane Smith", status: "Offline")
        ]

        var body: some View {
            List(users, id: \.name) { user in
                HStack {
                    Image(systemName: "person.circle")
                    VStack(alignment: .leading) {
                        Text(user.name)
                            .font(.headline)
                        Text(user.status)
                            .font(.subheadline)
                            .foregroundColor(.gray)
                    }
                }
            }
        }
    }
```

This example uses a `HStack` and `VStack` to create a custom layout for each list item, including an icon and two text elements.

# Building Complex, Scalable Lists and Sections

As your app grows, you'll need to handle more complex data structures and organize large lists into sections. SwiftUI provides easy-to-use tools for creating sectioned and grouped lists.

### Grouping Data with Sections

You can organize a list into sections based on a particular property, such as categories or dates. Each section can have a header and its own list of items.

```
struct SectionedListView: View {
```

```
let items = [
    "Fruit": ["Apple", "Banana", "Orange"],
    "Vegetables": ["Carrot", "Lettuce", "Tomato"]
]

var body: some View {
    List {
        ForEach(items.keys.sorted(), id: \.self) { section in
            Section(header: Text(section)) {
                ForEach(items[section]!, id: \.self) { item in
                    Text(item)
                }
            }
        }
    }
}
```

This structure allows you to create a dynamic list grouped into sections, each with its own header.

**Handling Large Data Efficiently**

For large datasets, performance becomes critical. SwiftUI's `List` view is optimized for performance, but when dealing with large datasets, consider using techniques like pagination, lazy loading, or asynchronous data fetching to ensure smooth user experience.

## Managing State in Large Data-Driven Views

When building apps with large datasets, managing state efficiently is crucial. SwiftUI offers a variety of tools for managing state in views that require frequent updates.

**Using State and Binding in Complex Views**

In large, dynamic views, you may need to manage the state of individual components. SwiftUI provides tools like `@State`, `@Binding`, and `@ObservedObject` to manage state in your views and ensure they update correctly.

```
struct ItemDetailView: View {
    @State private var isFavorite = false

    var body: some View {
        Button(action: {
            isFavorite.toggle()
        }) {
            Text(isFavorite ? "Remove from Favorites" : "Add to Favorites")
        }
    }
}
```

By utilizing `@State` and `@Binding`, you can manage changes in state and ensure that the UI reflects the updated state.

## Custom Animations and Transitions

Animations and transitions are essential for creating a polished and dynamic user experience. SwiftUI provides a powerful animation API that allows you to easily create custom animations and transitions.

### Creating Complex Animations with SwiftUI's Animation API

SwiftUI offers a simple and declarative syntax for defining animations. You can animate properties such as position, scale, rotation, and color. Here's an example of animating a view's opacity:

```
struct FadeView: View {
    @State private var isVisible = false
```

```
var body: some View {
  Text("Hello, World!")
    .opacity(isVisible ? 1 : 0)
    .onTapGesture {
      withAnimation {
        isVisible.toggle()
      }
    }
}
}
```

In this example, the opacity of the text changes when tapped, creating a

fade-in/fade-out effect.

**Customizing Transitions Between Views**

Transitions control how views appear and disappear from the screen. SwiftUI's transition API allows you to create a variety of effects, from simple fades to complex custom animations.

```
struct CustomTransitionView: View {
  @State private var showText = false

  var body: some View {
    VStack {
      if showText {
        Text("Here is some text!")
          .transition(.scale)
      }

      Button("Toggle Text") {
        withAnimation {
          showText.toggle()
        }
```

```
        }
      }
    }
}
```

This example creates a smooth transition for the text using a `scale` transition.

# Chapter 8

# Handling Multimedia and Advanced UI Elements

Creating applications that handle multimedia, including audio, video, and images, requires careful consideration of both performance and user experience. As an iOS developer, integrating rich media and implementing advanced UI components is essential for building feature-rich applications that are engaging and interactive. In this chapter, we will cover the integration of multimedia elements, advanced image handling, and gesture recognition, providing you with the tools to build sophisticated, responsive, and user-centric interfaces.

## Integrating Audio and Video into iOS Apps

Media content, including audio and video, plays a pivotal role in many modern applications, from media players to social apps. Integrating audio and video efficiently enhances the app's interactivity and appeal.

### Working with AVFoundation for Media Playback

AVFoundation is the primary framework for handling audio and video playback on iOS. It provides a set of powerful APIs for managing and controlling media playback.

To start, you can use `AVPlayer` to play audio and video files. Here's a basic example of how to play an audio file:

import AVFoundation

```swift
class AudioPlayer {

    var player: AVPlayer?

    func playAudio(fileURL: URL) {

        player = AVPlayer(url: fileURL)

        player?.play()

    }

    func stopAudio() {

        player?.pause()

    }

}
```

In this example, `AVPlayer` is initialized with a URL pointing to the audio file, and playback is started with the `play()` method. Similarly, video playback can be managed using `AVPlayerViewController` for more complex scenarios involving video files.

**Handling Video Playback**

For video playback, AVFoundation provides the `AVPlayerViewController`, which offers a ready-made interface for playing video content. This controller can be easily presented in a SwiftUI-based app using `UIViewControllerRepresentable`.

```
import AVKit

struct VideoPlayerView: View {
    let url: URL

    var body: some View {
        AVPlayerViewControllerRepresented(player: AVPlayer(url: url))
            .frame(width: 300, height: 200)
    }
}

struct AVPlayerViewControllerRepresented: UIViewControllerRepresentable {
    var player: AVPlayer

    func makeUIViewController(context: Context) -> AVPlayerViewController {
        let controller = AVPlayerViewController()
        controller.player = player
        return controller
    }

    func updateUIViewController(_ uiViewController: AVPlayerViewController,
context: Context) {
```

```
        // Nothing to update here

    }

}
```

This example shows how to integrate `AVPlayerViewController` with SwiftUI by using `UIViewControllerRepresentable`, allowing you to easily embed video playback within your views.

## Handling Real-Time Audio Streaming and Recording

For applications that require real-time audio processing or streaming, handling audio input and output in real time is crucial. Whether you are building a music streaming app or a voice recording app, you need to manage audio streams efficiently.

### Real-Time Audio Streaming

To stream audio in real-time, you can use `AVPlayer` along with a media URL to fetch and play audio from a live stream. The audio is fetched from the stream and played through the player:

```
func startAudioStreaming(streamURL: URL) {

    let player = AVPlayer(url: streamURL)

    player.play()

}
```

### Audio Recording with AVAudioRecorder

For recording audio, `AVAudioRecorder` provides the necessary functionality. By configuring the recorder with the correct settings, you can record high-quality audio.

```
import AVFoundation


class AudioRecorder {

    var recorder: AVAudioRecorder?


    func startRecording() {

        let fileURL = getAudioFileURL()

        let settings: [String: Any] = [

            AVFormatIDKey: Int(kAudioFormatMPEG4AAC),

            AVSampleRateKey: 44100,

            AVNumberOfChannelsKey: 1

        ]


        do {

            recorder = try AVAudioRecorder(url: fileURL, settings: settings)

            recorder?.record()

        } catch {

            print("Error starting recording: \(error)")

        }
```

```
    }


    func stopRecording() {

        recorder?.stop()

    }



    private func getAudioFileURL() -> URL {

        let documentsDirectory = FileManager.default.urls(for: .documentDirectory,
in: .userDomainMask)[0]

        return documentsDirectory.appendingPathComponent("audioRecording.m4a")

    }

}
```

In this example, we configure the audio recorder with settings that specify the audio format, sample rate, and number of channels. The `startRecording()` function begins capturing audio, and the `stopRecording()` function halts the recording.

## Advanced Image Handling in SwiftUI

SwiftUI provides powerful tools for working with images, allowing you to easily display, manipulate, and optimize images in your app. Efficient image handling can make a significant difference in both the performance and user experience of your application.

### Optimizing Image Loading and Caching Techniques

When working with images, especially high-resolution ones, it's crucial to optimize loading times and manage memory effectively. To handle large or remote images, you can implement caching and asynchronous loading.

SwiftUI provides the `AsyncImage` view for fetching images asynchronously. To improve performance, consider using caching mechanisms to prevent repeated network calls.

```
struct CachedImageView: View {

    @State private var imageData: Data? = nil

    let url: URL


    var body: some View {
        if let data = imageData, let uiImage = UIImage(data: data) {
            Image(uiImage: uiImage)
                .resizable()
                .scaledToFit()
        } else {
            ProgressView()
                .onAppear {
                    loadImage()
                }
        }
    }
}
```

```swift
private func loadImage() {

    if let cachedData = ImageCache.shared.get(forKey: url.absoluteString) {

        imageData = cachedData

        return

    }


    URLSession.shared.dataTask(with: url) { data, _, _ in

        if let data = data {

            ImageCache.shared.set(data, forKey: url.absoluteString)

            DispatchQueue.main.async {

                imageData = data

            }

        }

    }.resume()

}
}


class ImageCache {

    static let shared = ImageCache()

    private var cache = NSCache<NSString, NSData>()
```

```
func get(forKey key: String) -> Data? {

    return cache.object(forKey: key as NSString) as Data?

}


func set(_ data: Data, forKey key: String) {

    cache.setObject(data as NSData, forKey: key as NSString)

}

}
```

In this implementation, `CachedImageView` asynchronously loads an image and caches it for future use, reducing network requests and improving app performance.

**Working with Images in Different Resolutions**

Handling images for various screen sizes and resolutions is crucial in modern app development. iOS devices feature different screen resolutions, and it's essential to display images that look crisp and clear on all devices. Using image assets with the appropriate resolution for each screen density (1x, 2x, 3x) ensures optimal quality.

For this purpose, SwiftUI automatically handles different resolutions when you add images to the asset catalog. However, if you need to handle multiple resolutions manually, you can use `UIImage` and its methods for dynamic resolution handling.

let image = UIImage(named: "imageName")!

let scale = UIScreen.main.scale

let resizedImage = image.resized(to: CGSize(width: 200, height: 200 * scale))

```
extension UIImage {

    func resized(to newSize: CGSize) -> UIImage {

        UIGraphicsBeginImageContextWithOptions(newSize, false, self.scale)

        self.draw(in: CGRect(origin: .zero, size: newSize))

        let resizedImage = UIGraphicsGetImageFromCurrentImageContext()

        UIGraphicsEndImageContext()

        return resizedImage!

    }

}
```

This method dynamically resizes images based on the screen's resolution.

## Custom Gesture Recognition and Interaction

Gesture recognition is a vital aspect of interactive UIs, enabling users to interact naturally with your application. SwiftUI offers powerful tools for recognizing and responding to gestures, such as taps, swipes, and pinches.

### Building Interactive UIs with SwiftUI Gestures

SwiftUI provides several built-in gestures, including `TapGesture`, `DragGesture`, and `MagnificationGesture`, that make it simple to add interactive behavior to your views.

Here's an example of implementing a simple tap gesture:

```
struct TapGestureView: View {

    @State private var tapped = false
```

```swift
var body: some View {

    Text(tapped ? "Tapped!" : "Tap Me")

        .padding()

        .background(Color.blue)

        .foregroundColor(.white)

        .cornerRadius(10)

        .onTapGesture {

            tapped.toggle()

        }

    }

}
```

In this example, the `onTapGesture` modifier allows the view to respond to taps, toggling the `tapped` state and updating the UI accordingly.

**Advanced Gesture-Based Animations**

Gestures can also be combined with animations to create dynamic and interactive user interfaces. For example, you can use a drag gesture to move an object on the screen and animate the movement.

```swift
struct DragAnimationView: View {

    @State private var offset = CGSize.zero
```

```
var body: some View {

  Text("Drag Me!")

    .padding()

    .background(Color.green)

    .foregroundColor(.white)

    .cornerRadius(8)

    .offset(offset)

    .gesture(

      DragGesture()

        .onChanged { value in

          withAnimation {

            offset = value.translation

          }

        }

        .onEnded { _ in

          withAnimation {

            offset = .zero

          }

        }

    )

}
```

```
}
```

In this case, the `DragGesture` is combined with animation to create a smooth and interactive dragging effect.

# Chapter 9

# Testing, Debugging, and Performance Optimization

Developing a visually appealing and functionally robust iOS app is only half the journey. The real test of an application lies in its stability, efficiency, and resilience in real-world scenarios. SwiftUI and Xcode offer powerful tools to test code logic, examine user interfaces under different conditions, and diagnose potential performance bottlenecks. A comprehensive approach to testing, debugging, and performance tuning is essential for ensuring an app not only works but works well.

## Unit and UI Testing with Xcode and SwiftUI

Xcode supports two distinct types of testing workflows: **unit testing** and **UI testing**. These allow developers to isolate logic-based flaws and catch regressions in user-facing components before shipping updates. Swift's built-in XCTest framework provides the foundation for writing test cases that confirm expected behavior across modules.

### Writing and Running Unit Tests in Swift

Unit testing targets individual components like classes, structs, or functions. This form of testing verifies that each part of your code performs as expected under defined conditions.

### Key Concepts

- **XCTestCase**: All test classes inherit from this base class.

- **setUp() and tearDown()**: These are used to initialize and clean up resources before and after each test method.

- **Assertions**: XCTest provides various assertions such as `XCTAssertEqual`, `XCTAssertTrue`, and `XCTAssertThrowsError` to verify outcomes.

**Sample Unit Test**

```
import XCTest

@testable import YourAppModule


class MathUtilityTests: XCTestCase {


    func testAddition() {

        let result = MathUtility.add(3, 5)

        XCTAssertEqual(result, 8, "Addition function should return 8 when adding 3 and 5")

    }

}
```

Run these tests using the **Test Navigator** (⌘ + 6 in Xcode) or by selecting Product > Test in the menu bar.

**UI Testing: Automating SwiftUI View Tests**

UI testing verifies how user interactions behave on screen. It simulates user actions like taps, swipes, and typing, ensuring the user interface responds correctly under varying scenarios.

**Creating UI Tests**

1. Enable UI testing when creating a new test target.

2. Import the `XCTest` framework and reference `XCUIApplication` to launch the app.

3. Use XCUIElement queries to locate buttons, text fields, and views.

```
func testLoginButtonExists() {

    let app = XCUIApplication()

    app.launch()

    let loginButton = app.buttons["Login"]

    XCTAssertTrue(loginButton.exists)

}
```

UI tests can be executed on simulators or physical devices and are ideal for regression testing on larger apps with multiple views.

---

# Debugging Techniques for Complex iOS Applications

Even experienced developers face bugs that are hard to trace. Knowing how to use the debugging capabilities of Xcode makes it easier to pinpoint problems without wasting time on guesswork.

**Leveraging Xcode's Debugging Tools**

Xcode offers real-time insights through breakpoints, memory graphs, logging, and symbolic debugging.

### Breakpoints

Strategic breakpoints pause execution at specific lines, allowing inspection of variable values and program flow.

- **Conditional breakpoints**: Trigger only when a condition is met.

- **Symbolic breakpoints**: Trigger on function calls, useful for observing UIKit lifecycle events.

### LLDB Debugger

Use LLDB (Low-Level Debugger) in the console to evaluate expressions or change values at runtime.

po myVariable

expression myInt = 5

### Debug Navigator

This window provides a timeline of CPU, memory, and thread activity. Red flags in this area often point to leaks, excessive CPU usage, or main-thread blocking.

---

# Handling Performance Issues and Memory Leaks

Poor performance often stems from inefficient code, redundant rendering, or memory leaks. Regular profiling is key to catching these issues early.

## Using Instruments for Performance Analysis

Xcode Instruments lets you inspect an app's behavior through various profiling tools.

- **Time Profiler**: Detects CPU-heavy functions and stack traces.

- **Allocations**: Shows memory usage by objects and their lifecycles.

- **Leaks**: Identifies memory blocks that are no longer referenced but not released.

To open Instruments: Product > Profile or use shortcut ⌘ + I.

**Fixing Memory Leaks**

Leaks in SwiftUI often happen due to strong reference cycles between view models and views. Use weak or unowned references when appropriate, especially when closures or delegates are involved.

class ViewModel {

   weak var delegate: SomeDelegate?

}

---

# Optimizing SwiftUI Code for Performance

SwiftUI's declarative syntax can sometimes lead to unnecessary view re-renders, especially when state changes aren't properly scoped.

**Use of `@State`, `@Binding`, and `@ObservedObject`**

Improper state management causes views to redraw more than necessary.

- Use `@State` for local view properties.

- Use `@Binding` when passing state down to child views.

- Use `@ObservedObject` for shared data between views.

- Use `@StateObject` to avoid recreation of the view model across re-renders.

**Avoiding Overhead**

- Use `.drawingGroup()` sparingly—it rasterizes the view, which can slow down rendering if misused.

- Minimize layout recalculations by avoiding deep nesting of `VStacks` and `HStacks`.

- Use `.equatable()` and `.id()` modifiers to help SwiftUI understand when not to redraw a view.

# Best Practices for Reducing App Load Time

Application launch time directly affects the user's perception of quality. SwiftUI apps can be tuned to become responsive from the first tap.

### Cold vs Warm Launch

- **Cold launch**: App starts from scratch—ensure minimal tasks are performed here.

- **Warm launch**: App resumes from background—avoid unnecessary reset logic.

**Optimization Techniques**

- Defer non-critical tasks using `DispatchQueue.main.asyncAfter`.

- Avoid heavy computations in `AppDelegate` or `SceneDelegate`.

- Lazy-load views and data only when needed.

- Use lightweight assets or compress images.

# Memory Management in SwiftUI Applications

Swift has a robust memory management system based on Automatic Reference Counting (ARC), but SwiftUI's abstraction requires developers to be extra mindful of how views and view models interact.

## Common Pitfalls

- Retain cycles from closures referencing `self` strongly.

- Holding strong references to views that persist longer than needed.

- Overuse of `.onAppear` without paired `.onDisappear`.

**Avoiding Retain Cycles**

Use `[weak self]` inside closures to prevent unintentional memory retention.

somePublisher

```
.sink { [weak self] value in

    self?.handle(value)

}
```

**Monitoring with Memory Graph**

The Memory Graph Debugger in Xcode visually shows retained objects. Leaked objects are usually marked with a yellow flag.

# Chapter 10

# Deploying Your iOS App

Building an iOS app involves more than writing code and polishing interfaces. The deployment phase is where technical implementation meets operational execution. Developers must understand how to prepare an application for submission, configure essential metadata, follow established distribution procedures, and implement automation pipelines to maintain reliability. This chapter offers a structured breakdown of the deployment process using publicly available tools and information, ensuring a smooth transition from development to user distribution.

## Preparing Your App for the App Store

Before submission, every application must meet quality standards and function consistently across devices. Preparing your app involves technical readiness and compliance with platform expectations.

**Checklist Before Submission**

- **Ensure stability**: The app must not crash under any user interaction.

- **Remove debugging tools**: All logs, breakpoints, and test interfaces should be stripped.

- **Confirm UI compliance**: Avoid unreadable text, offscreen elements, or inconsistent layout on different devices.

- **Accessibility**: Support Dynamic Type, VoiceOver, and proper semantic labeling of elements.

**App Store Assets**

In addition to the build itself, you must upload supporting material:

- **App Icon**: Provided in multiple resolutions (up to 1024x1024 px).

- **Screenshots**: Specific to each device size (iPhone SE, iPhone 14 Pro, iPad, etc.).

- **App Previews (optional)**: Short videos demonstrating app functionality.

Use Xcode's **Archive and Distribute** workflow to compile the final product. Archiving bundles all dependencies, resources, and compiled code into a format suitable for upload to App Store Connect.

---

# Managing App Metadata and Certificates

App Store Connect is the portal where developers submit apps, manage profiles, and track performance. Metadata and certificates form the backbone of this process.

**Metadata Setup**

When registering an app in App Store Connect:

- **Name**: The public-facing title.

- **Subtitle and description**: Provide clear, concise information about features and usage.

- **Keywords**: These improve search relevance.

- **Support URL and marketing URL**: Required fields, even if you use placeholder links.

### Certificates, Identifiers, and Profiles

Three components govern the security and identity of your app:

1. **Certificates**: Used to sign builds. You'll need:

   - A **Development Certificate** for testing.

   - A **Distribution Certificate** for production deployment.

2. **App Identifiers (Bundle ID)**: Unique reverse-DNS string to identify your app.

3. **Provisioning Profiles**: These link your app identifier with the right certificate and entitlements.

Use Xcode's **Signing & Capabilities** section to automate much of this setup. Alternatively, manage manually using the **Apple Developer Portal**.

---

## App Store Submission Guidelines and Common Pitfalls

Apple maintains specific guidelines developers must follow to avoid rejection. These guidelines address performance, privacy, design, and legal concerns.

### Common Rejection Reasons

- **Crashes on launch**: Uncaught exceptions or missing resources.

- **Privacy issues**: Use of private APIs or missing permission descriptions in Info.plist.

- **Incomplete metadata**: Vague descriptions or screenshots that don't reflect actual app behavior.

- **Misleading claims**: Inaccurate marketing language or unsubstantiated health-related claims.

- **Broken links or dead-end workflows**.

Always test your app thoroughly on different devices and OS versions. Ensure you include permission usage strings (e.g., `NSCameraUsageDescription`) to avoid runtime crashes.

---

## Distributing Beta Versions with TestFlight

Before releasing your app to the public, distributing a beta version is essential for real-user feedback. Apple provides **TestFlight**, a pre-release testing platform that integrates directly with App Store Connect.

**Uploading to TestFlight**

1. Archive your app in Xcode.

2. Use **Product > Archive**, then **Distribute App > App Store Connect > Upload**.

3. Once processed, your build appears in the **TestFlight** tab in App Store Connect.

**Managing Testers**

- **Internal testers**: Up to 100 team members using their Apple ID.

- **External testers**: Up to 10,000 individuals via public or private invitation.

- Create testing groups, assign builds, and include testing instructions and notes.

---

# Configuring TestFlight for Feedback and Testing

Collecting quality feedback from beta testers depends on how well you structure the process.

### Setting Expectations

- Include clear update notes with each beta build.

- Provide testers with scenarios to explore, such as onboarding, payments, or login flows.

- Ask for structured feedback (e.g., reproducible bugs, performance impressions).

Testers can send feedback directly through the TestFlight app, which captures screenshots, crash logs, and device diagnostics.

### Monitor Build Expiration

TestFlight builds expire after 90 days. Continuously monitor their availability and upload fresh builds as needed, especially during long beta cycles.

---

# Managing Beta Builds and Distribution

Proper build management prevents confusion and ensures testers always use the most up-to-date version.

**Build Labels and Versioning**

- **Semantic versioning** (e.g., 1.2.0) helps distinguish between major, minor, and patch-level changes.

- Increment the **build number** with every upload to App Store Connect.

- Include release notes summarizing what's new or fixed.

**Testing Across Variants**

- Test with both debug and release configurations.

- Validate behavior across different devices, orientations, and accessibility settings.

- Ensure new features don't regress existing functionality.

# Continuous Integration and Deployment for SwiftUI Projects

Automating your development workflow improves reliability and reduces manual error. Continuous integration (CI) and continuous deployment (CD) ensure every code change is tested and built consistently.

**Setting Up CI/CD Pipelines with Xcode**

Xcode Cloud (or alternatives like GitHub Actions and Bitrise) enables build automation:

- **Triggers**: Pipelines begin after pushing to the main branch or opening a pull request.

- **Build and Test Stages**: Ensure the project compiles and tests pass before deployment.

- **Artifact Storage**: Archives builds or test results for review.

Basic CI/CD setup with GitHub Actions:

```
name: iOS CI


on:

 push:

  branches: [ main ]


jobs:

 build:

  runs-on: macos-latest


  steps:

   - uses: actions/checkout@v2

   - name: Set up Xcode

    uses: maxim-lobanov/setup-xcode@v1

    with:
```

```
    xcode-version: '15.0'

  - name: Build and Test

    run: xcodebuild test -scheme YourApp -destination 'platform=iOS
Simulator,name=iPhone 14'
```

This configuration automatically tests your app whenever new code is pushed.

---

## Automating Build and Test Processes

Automation ensures that quality gates are always applied and that every update is predictable. This helps catch issues early and maintains consistent build behavior.

**Benefits of Automation**

- **Early bug detection** through regular testing.

- **Reduced manual effort** for repetitive tasks like code signing or archiving.

- **Reliable deployment** of beta and production builds without human error.

**Tools for Automation**

- **Fastlane**: Automates certificate management, screenshots, builds, and uploads.

- **Xcode Server**: Built into Xcode for macOS-based CI.

- **GitHub Actions**: Supports custom scripts for testing, linting, and deployment.

Example Fastlane configuration for deploying to TestFlight:

```
default_platform(:ios)


platform :ios do

  desc "Push a new beta build to TestFlight"

  lane :beta do

    build_app(scheme: "YourApp")

    upload_to_testflight

  end

end
```

Execute this with `fastlane beta`, and your app will be built and uploaded without needing to open Xcode.

# Chapter 11

# Advanced Topics in iOS Development

Advancing in iOS development requires expanding your skill set beyond the basics. This chapter explores sophisticated areas such as adapting SwiftUI for macOS and watchOS applications, selecting appropriate architectural patterns like MVVM and VIPER, and integrating augmented reality experiences using ARKit with SwiftUI. Each section provides insights and guidelines to enhance your app development proficiency.

---

## SwiftUI for macOS and watchOS Development

### Adapting SwiftUI for macOS Applications

SwiftUI enables developers to create applications across Apple's platforms using a unified codebase. When targeting macOS, it's essential to understand the platform's unique characteristics and user expectations.

### Key Considerations for macOS Development

- **User Interface Paradigms**: macOS applications often feature resizable windows, menus, and toolbars. Ensure your SwiftUI layouts adapt seamlessly to various window sizes and support standard macOS controls.

- **File Management**: macOS users anticipate robust file handling capabilities. Implement features like drag-and-drop, open/save panels, and integration with the Finder.

- **Keyboard and Mouse Input**: Unlike touch-centric iOS devices, macOS relies heavily on keyboard and mouse interactions. Design your app to respond appropriately to these input methods.

To start a macOS project with SwiftUI:

1. **Create a New macOS Project**: In Xcode, select "App" under the macOS tab when creating a new project. Ensure SwiftUI is chosen as the interface.

2. **Leverage Platform-Specific Views**: While SwiftUI provides many cross-platform components, some views are exclusive to macOS. Utilize these to enhance the user experience.

3. **Testing**: Regularly test your application on different macOS devices to ensure compatibility and responsiveness.

For a comprehensive guide on creating macOS apps with SwiftUI, refer to Apple's official tutorial. citeturn0search0

**Developing watchOS Apps with SwiftUI**

The compact nature of Apple Watch necessitates a streamlined approach to app design. SwiftUI simplifies the development process for watchOS by offering a declarative syntax that aligns well with the device's constraints.

**Steps to Develop a watchOS App**

1. **Add a watchOS Target**: In your existing Xcode project, add a new target specifically for watchOS. This action generates the necessary files and groups for your watch app. citeturn0search1

2. **Design for Small Screens**: Prioritize essential information and interactions due to limited screen real estate. Use concise text and simple layouts.

3. **Utilize Watch-Specific Features**: Incorporate elements like the Digital Crown, haptic feedback, and complications to enhance user engagement.

4. **Optimize Performance**: Given the hardware limitations, ensure your app is efficient in both performance and energy consumption.

Apple's SwiftUI tutorials provide detailed instructions on creating watchOS apps. citeturn0search1

---

## App Architectures: MVVM, VIPER, and More

Choosing an appropriate architecture is crucial for building scalable and maintainable applications. Two prevalent patterns in iOS development are MVVM (Model-View-ViewModel) and VIPER (View-Interactor-Presenter-Entity-Router).

**Choosing the Right Architecture for Your App**

- **MVVM**: This pattern facilitates a clear separation between the user interface and business logic. The ViewModel acts as an intermediary, managing data transformations and state. MVVM is particularly compatible with SwiftUI's declarative nature.

- **VIPER**: Standing for View, Interactor, Presenter, Entity, and Router, VIPER offers a highly modular structure. Each component has a distinct responsibility, promoting testability and scalability. However, its complexity may be overkill for simpler projects.

When deciding on an architecture:

- **Project Scope**: For small to medium projects, MVVM's simplicity may suffice. Larger, more complex applications might benefit from VIPER's rigorous separation of concerns.

- **Team Collaboration**: A well-defined architecture can streamline teamwork by clearly delineating responsibilities.

- **Future Maintenance**: Consider how easily the app can be extended or modified in the future.

For an in-depth comparison between VIPER and MVVM, refer to this article. citeturn0search2

**Building Scalable and Maintainable Apps**

Regardless of the chosen architecture, adhere to best practices to ensure your app remains scalable and maintainable:

- **Modularity**: Design components that can be developed, tested, and updated independently.

- **Code Reusability**: Write generic and reusable code to minimize duplication and potential errors.

- **Comprehensive Testing**: Implement unit and integration tests to catch issues early and facilitate refactoring.

- **Clear Documentation**: Maintain thorough documentation to assist current and future developers in understanding the codebase.

# SwiftUI and Augmented Reality (ARKit)

Augmented Reality (AR) enhances user experiences by overlaying digital content onto the real world. Combining SwiftUI with ARKit allows developers to create immersive and interactive applications.

**Introduction to ARKit for iOS Development**

ARKit is Apple's framework for building AR experiences on iOS devices. It provides tools for motion tracking, environmental understanding, and light estimation, enabling the integration of virtual objects into real-world scenes.

To integrate ARKit with SwiftUI:

1. **Set Up the Project**: Create a new Xcode project and ensure your device supports ARKit.

2. **Import Necessary Frameworks**: Import ARKit and, optionally, RealityKit for rendering 3D content.

3. **Create an ARView**: Use `ARView` from RealityKit as the container for AR content.

4. **Configure AR Session**: Set up an `ARSession` with the desired configuration, such as world tracking.

5. **Add Virtual Content**: Place 3D models or other virtual objects into the AR scene.

For a step-by-step tutorial on building an interactive AR experience with SwiftUI, consult this resource. citeturn0search3

**Creating Immersive AR Experiences with SwiftUI**

To develop compelling AR applications:

- **Realistic Rendering**: Use high-quality 3D models and textures to make virtual objects blend seamlessly with the real environment.

- **User Interaction**: Implement gestures and controls that allow users to manipulate virtual objects naturally.

- **Environmental Understanding**: Leverage ARKit's capabilities to detect surfaces, objects, and lighting conditions, enhancing the realism of the AR experience.

- **Performance Optimization**: AR applications can be resource-intensive. Optimize your code and assets to maintain smooth performance and conserve battery life.

For additional guidance on creating AR apps with SwiftUI and RealityKit, refer to this tutorial. citeturn0search7

# Chapter 12

# The Future of iOS Development with Swift and SwiftUI

The landscape of iOS development is continually evolving, driven by technological advancements and changing user expectations. This chapter explores emerging trends, the integration of artificial intelligence, the expansion of SwiftUI across platforms, and strategies for continuous learning to remain at the forefront of the field.

---

## Emerging Trends in iOS Development

### AI and Machine Learning Integration with CoreML

Artificial intelligence (AI) and machine learning (ML) have become integral to modern app development, enabling features such as personalized recommendations, voice recognition, and predictive analytics. Apple's CoreML framework facilitates the integration of ML models into iOS applications, allowing developers to create intelligent and responsive apps.

### Integrating CoreML into SwiftUI Applications

To incorporate a CoreML model into a SwiftUI project:

1. **Obtain a Trained Model**: Utilize tools like Create ML to develop a custom model or acquire pre-trained models from reputable sources.

2. **Add the Model to Your Project**: Import the `.mlmodel` file into your Xcode project. Xcode will automatically generate a Swift interface for the model.

3. **Utilize the Model in Your Code**: Instantiate the model and provide it with appropriate input data to receive predictions.

For a comprehensive tutorial on connecting SwiftUI to CoreML, refer to Hacking with Swift.

**Integrating SwiftUI with Cloud Services and Data Sync**

Modern applications often require seamless data synchronization across devices. Integrating SwiftUI with cloud services like CloudKit enables real-time data syncing, enhancing user experience.

**Syncing Data with CloudKit in SwiftUI**

To synchronize data using CloudKit:

1. **Enable iCloud Capabilities**: In your Xcode project settings, activate iCloud and select CloudKit.

2. **Configure the Data Model**: Define your data model using SwiftData, ensuring it aligns with CloudKit's requirements.

3. **Implement Data Synchronization**: Utilize SwiftData's integration with CloudKit to manage data syncing across devices.

For detailed guidance on syncing SwiftData with CloudKit, consult Hacking with Swift.

---

# SwiftUI Beyond iOS: Extending to iPadOS, macOS, and More

**Cross-Platform Development with SwiftUI**

SwiftUI's declarative syntax and unified framework facilitate the development of applications that run seamlessly across multiple Apple platforms, including iOS, iPadOS, macOS, and watchOS. This approach streamlines the development process and ensures a consistent user experience.

**Building Universal Apps for the Apple Ecosystem**

To create a universal app:

1. **Set Up a Multiplatform Project**: In Xcode, select the multiplatform template to initiate a project that targets multiple platforms.

2. **Design Adaptive Interfaces**: Utilize SwiftUI's responsive layout system to ensure the interface adapts to various screen sizes and orientations.

3. **Handle Platform-Specific Features**: Implement conditional code to address functionalities unique to each platform.

Apple's Food Truck tutorial provides an example of building a multiplatform SwiftUI application.

---

# Staying Ahead: Continuous Learning and Community Involvement

**Leveraging SwiftUI and Xcode Resources**

Staying updated with the latest tools and frameworks is crucial for iOS developers. Apple offers a wealth of resources:

- **SwiftUI Tutorials**: Apple's SwiftUI Tutorials cover various aspects of SwiftUI development.

- **Xcode Documentation**: The <u>Xcode Resources</u> page provides insights into utilizing Xcode effectively.

**Engaging with Developer Communities and Staying Updated**

Active participation in developer communities fosters knowledge sharing and professional growth:

- **Online Forums**: Platforms like the <u>Apple Developer Forums</u> facilitate discussions and problem-solving among developers.

- **Conferences and Workshops**: Events such as <u>WWDC</u> offer opportunities to learn about the latest developments and network with peers.

- **Open-Source Contributions**: Engaging with open-source projects allows developers to collaborate and stay informed about emerging trends.

By integrating AI and ML capabilities, embracing cross-platform development with SwiftUI, and committing to continuous learning, developers can create innovative and versatile applications that meet the evolving demands of users.

# Conclusion

## The Road Ahead for iOS Developers

iOS development has moved far beyond the days of imperative UIKit and has matured into a fast-moving field shaped by a modern, declarative approach through SwiftUI. The combination of Swift and SwiftUI is not simply a trend; it is the default method for building polished, consistent, and maintainable applications across Apple platforms. As developers adopt this unified approach, the focus naturally shifts toward writing cleaner, more modular code, designing scalable architectures, and delivering high-quality user experiences with less boilerplate.

Staying relevant in this field no longer means mastering just the syntax. It means developing a critical mindset toward how components are reused, how data is passed and observed, and how real-world requirements translate into app behavior. The more Swift and SwiftUI evolve, the more developers are required to understand the underlying design philosophies—things like data-driven UI, state consistency, modular structures, and system-driven layouts.

Apple's direction is clear: they continue to emphasize simplicity, safety, and seamless integration across their devices. This doesn't mean things are getting easier; rather, the expectation now is for developers to produce robust and elegant applications that function across iPhones, iPads, watches, and desktops without losing performance or polish. For developers willing to adapt and expand their skillset, this shift opens the door to more opportunities than ever before.

## Next Steps in Mastering Swift and SwiftUI

### 1. Deepen Your Understanding of Swift's Capabilities

After building a strong foundation, the next logical step is to master the deeper language features that separate average apps from great ones. This includes:

- Understanding **protocol-oriented programming**

- Mastering **concurrency using Swift's structured concurrency model** (`async/await`)

- Writing **generic code** that's clean and reusable

- Implementing **custom Combine publishers and operators**

- Building **custom Swift packages** to modularize and reuse code

Practicing these topics in the context of real applications is the only reliable way to internalize them.

**2. Level Up Your SwiftUI Skills Through Projects**

Knowledge means little without practice. Developing a series of real-world projects, each with increasing complexity, forces you to solve practical UI and data challenges. Consider building apps that:

- Persist and sync data using SwiftData and CloudKit

- Render dynamic and deeply nested lists

- Support offline mode and seamless reactivity

- Leverage animation APIs to guide user interaction naturally

- Use `NavigationStack`, `ScrollViewReader`, `matchedGeometryEffect`, and `Canvas` for advanced UI experiences

As you do, challenge yourself to abstract views, isolate responsibilities, and test interactions thoroughly.

### 3. Refine Architectural Thinking

Apps grow in complexity. When they do, code that once worked well becomes hard to maintain. That's where architectural discipline makes a difference. Study and apply patterns such as:

- **MVVM with ObservableObject and @StateObject**

- **Dependency Injection**

- **Unidirectional data flow (inspired by Redux or The Composable Architecture)**

- **Data and domain layering for separation of concerns**

Instead of copying what you see online, take time to understand **why** these patterns exist. That insight will help you design systems that are easier to reason about, easier to extend, and far less likely to break unexpectedly.

### 4. Stay Proactive with New APIs

Apple introduces dozens of APIs each year through their developer conferences and documentation. Staying current is a long-term commitment. To keep your toolset up-to-date:

- Explore new SwiftUI components introduced at each major version (e.g., `Observation`, `NavigationSplitView`, etc.)

- Integrate modern system features (like SharePlay, App Intents, TipKit, and WidgetKit)

- Participate in beta releases to prepare your codebase for OS updates

- Read technical breakdowns from reliable sources like <u>Swift by Sundell</u>, <u>Point-Free</u>, and <u>Hacking with Swift</u>

## 5. Contribute and Learn From the Community

The Swift and SwiftUI ecosystem is driven by thousands of independent developers. Participating in open-source projects or even just contributing issues or documentation improvements helps refine your judgment. You'll learn to:

- Read and understand large codebases

- Follow best practices for testing and documentation

- Contribute clean, reviewable pull requests

- Discuss and defend design choices

Communities on GitHub, Mastodon, Reddit, or dedicated Swift forums can be valuable sources of mentorship and feedback.

## 6. Prepare for Production-Ready Development

As your proficiency grows, so should your ability to ship reliable, secure, and maintainable apps. The transition from "just works" to "production-grade" involves mastering:

- **Accessibility** and supporting dynamic type, VoiceOver, and color contrast

- **Localization and internationalization** for global reach

- **Analytics** and usage tracking to understand user behavior

- **Crash monitoring tools** like Sentry or Firebase Crashlytics

- **CI/CD workflows** for faster iteration and deployment

- **App Store compliance** and efficient submission processes

These areas require attention to detail, long-term thinking, and a willingness to test extensively across devices, screen sizes, and real-world conditions.

# Appendices

## A. Swift Syntax Reference

Swift is a powerful and intuitive programming language developed by Apple for building applications across its platforms. This section provides an overview of essential Swift syntax to serve as a quick reference for developers.

**Constants and Variables**

**Constants**: Declared using the `let` keyword. Once set, their values cannot change.

let maximumLoginAttempts = 3

●

**Variables**: Declared using the `var` keyword. Their values can be modified after initial assignment.

var currentLoginAttempt = 0

●

**Data Types**

Swift offers various data types, including:

- **Integers**: Whole numbers, e.g., `Int`

- **Floating-Point Numbers**: Decimal numbers, e.g., `Double` and `Float`

- **Booleans**: `true` or `false`

- **Strings**: Textual data

Type inference allows Swift to deduce the type based on the assigned value:

let pi = 3.14159 // Inferred as Double

### Optionals

Optionals handle the absence of a value. An optional variable can either hold a value or be `nil`.

var optionalString: String? = "Hello"

optionalString = nil

To safely access the value of an optional, use optional binding:

if let unwrappedString = optionalString {

   print(unwrappedString)

} else {

   print("optionalString is nil")

}

### Control Flow

**Conditional Statements**: Use `if`, `else if`, and `else` to execute code based on conditions.

```
let temperature = 30
if temperature > 25 {
    print("It's a hot day.")
} else {
    print("It's a cool day.")
}
```

●

**Switch Statements**: Evaluate a value against multiple possible matching patterns.

```
let character = "a"
switch character {
case "a", "e", "i", "o", "u":
    print("\(character) is a vowel.")
default:
    print("\(character) is a consonant.")
}
```

●

● **Loops**:

`for-in` loop: Iterates over a sequence, such as items in an array.

```
let names = ["Alice", "Bob", "Charlie"]
for name in names {
```

```
    print(name)

}
```

○

`while` loop: Repeats a block of code while a condition is true.

```
 var count = 5

while count > 0 {

    print(count)

    count -= 1

}
```

○

**Functions**

Functions encapsulate reusable blocks of code.

```
func greet(person: String) -> String {

    return "Hello, \(person)!"

}

print(greet(person: "Anna"))
```

Functions can have multiple parameters and return multiple values using tuples.

```
func calculateStatistics(scores: [Int]) -> (min: Int, max: Int, sum: Int) {

    var min = scores[0]

    var max = scores[0]
```

```swift
    var sum = 0

    for score in scores {
        if score > max {
            max = score
        } else if score < min {
            min = score
        }
        sum += score
    }

    return (min, max, sum)
}
let statistics = calculateStatistics(scores: [5, 3, 100, 3, 9])
print(statistics.sum)
print(statistics.2)
```

**Closures**

Closures are self-contained blocks of functionality that can be passed around and used in your code.

```swift
let names = ["Chris", "Alex", "Ewa", "Barry", "Daniella"]
let reversedNames = names.sorted { $0 > $1 }
```

```
print(reversedNames)
```

**Structures and Classes**

**Structures**: Value types that encapsulate related properties and behaviors.

```
struct Resolution {
   var width = 0
   var height = 0
}
```

•

**Classes**: Reference types that support inheritance and type casting.

```
class Vehicle {
   var currentSpeed = 0.0
   var description: String {
      return "traveling at \(currentSpeed) miles per hour"
   }
}
```

•

For a comprehensive guide, refer to the Swift Programming Language Guide.

# B. Xcode Shortcuts and Tips

Efficient use of Xcode's shortcuts can significantly enhance productivity. Below is a selection of commonly used shortcuts:

## General

- **Preferences**: Command (⌘) + ,

- **Quick Open**: Shift (⇧) + Command (⌘) + O

- **Toggle Navigator**: Command (⌘) + 0

- **Toggle Utilities**: Option (⌥) + Command (⌘) + 0

- **Toggle Debug Area**: Shift (⇧) + Command (⌘) + Y

## Editing

- **Comment/Uncomment Line**: Command (⌘) + /

- **Duplicate Line**: Command (⌘) + D

- **Move Line Up/Down**: Option (⌥) + Command (⌘) + [ or ]

- **Indent Line**: Command (⌘) + ]

- **Unindent Line**: Command (⌘) + [

## Navigation

- **Jump to Definition**: Control (^) + Command (⌘) + J

- **Reveal in Project Navigator**: Shift (⇧) + Command (⌘) + J

- **Open Quickly**: Shift (⇧) + Command (⌘) + O

- **Go to Line**: Command (⌘) + L

**Build and Run**

- **Build Project**: Command (⌘) + B

- **Run Project**: Command (⌘) + R

- **Stop Execution**: Command (⌘) + .

- **Clean Build Folder**: Shift (⇧) + Command (⌘) + K

For a detailed list, refer to <u>Xcode Keyboard Shortcuts</u>.

Made in the USA
Columbia, SC
10 June 2025

59193747R00074